REINVENT YOURSELF

Strategies for Achieving Success in Every Area of Your Life

Karen,

There is greatness in you! Keep reaching for the stars. Love, Shirley

REINVENT YOURSELF

Strategies for Achieving
Success in Every Area
of Your Life

Dr. Shirley Davis
The Success Doctor™

ISBN 978-0-9896521-1-7

Editor: John Sprague Editorial

Cover design by: Christopher Haven

Interior designed by: Shirley E.M. Raybuck

Request for permission to make copies of any part of this book can be made to: www.drshirleydavis.com

Table of Contents

In order to receive maximum benefit of the concepts and strategies shared in this book a Companion Workbook is available. The *Reinvent Yourself Workbook* provides exercises, reflection questions, and personal assessments based on the material shared in this book. WHEN YOU SEE THIS SYMBOL **RYW**, IT MEANS THAT THERE IS A CORRESPONDING EXERCISE OR ACTIVITY FOR YOU TO COMPLETE. Working these exercises will help you to better integrate the material and focus your efforts towards reinventing yourself and achieving success in moving to the next level in your life. Order your copy today at **www.drshirleydavis.com/store**.

■ Acknowledgements/ Dedication

PEOPLE OFTEN ASK ME WHAT THE KEY TO MY SUCCESS IS. My answer is an emphatic: **"Family, Friends, and Faith."** For every important milestone in my life these three forces have been my anchor and my source of strength.

I want to especially acknowledge my dad and mom (Joseph and Shirley) and my three brothers (Craig, Joseph, and Jonathan) for your unwavering and unconditional love and for the closeness that we share as a family. You have always had my back. You have been my backbone and my cheering squad and it has propelled me to overcome every obstacle and adversity that I've faced and to step into my greatness with boldness, courage, and perseverance.

To my two BFFs (best friends forever) Neekey and Debbie, I thank God for allowing our paths to cross over 26 years ago. You have prayed for me, advised me, stood with me, and we've created great memories together. Thank you for accepting me as I am and for loving me anyway. I love you both deeply.

To my MINI-ME, my daughter and other best friend, Gabrielle Victoria. You are so gifted, talented and beautiful inside and out and I am SO proud of you. You are the wind beneath my wings and the reason that I work so hard in the pursuit of excellence. You are my Legacy and my Life and I love you forever. I can't wait to see you become an international singer and entertainer. You are on your way.

To my new husband (Terrell), thank you for being a part of the next chapter of my life. God has something great in store for us and I am blessed to be able to share my life with you, and with Brian and Terra. Together, we are all family.

And most importantly, I thank God for being my personal rock and my salvation. I will continue to serve you until the day I die and I am eternally grateful for your many blessings, favor, and your mercy and grace.

This book is dedicated to you all
with my sincerest love and thankfulness.

◼ Introduction

ARE YOU READY TO TAKE YOUR LIFE TO THE NEXT LEVEL? Are you ready to step into your greatness? Are you committed to walking in your purpose and making your life meaningful? If so, *Reinvent Yourself* is the right book for you. This is not a book about starting over. It's about reflecting on your life, reviewing where you are, where you've been, and where you're going. It's about revising your life strategy to help you reach your destiny.

As a success coach, I work with clients from all walks of life. They come to me from different ethnicities, ages, countries, and cultures. They have different educational backgrounds and religious beliefs. And they find themselves at different stages in their career or at different levels in their organizations. They come to me seeking strategies and solutions for living a life of purpose and fulfillment. Unfortunately, my time and schedule won't allow me to reach everyone on a one-on-one basis. So I wrote this book of coaching tips & best practices that I hope will help you find meaning and direction in your life.

So we'll cover a wide array of topics that when effectively addressed will help you enhance your career, your relationships, your finances, your professional endeavors, your spirituality, and, underlying it all, how you feel about yourself and how you make decisions.

In the first chapter, Redefining Success, I'm going to walk you through some ideas on what success looks like and what it really means to you. I will provide 20 self-assessment questions that I want you to reflect on. They will help you think about how you begin your journey.

In subsequent chapters I will cover things like how to reassess your purpose and vision; how to reprioritize your goals; how to retool your communication skills; how to rebuild your career; how to reevaluate your relationships; how to repair your finances; and ultimately, how to reclaim your personal power.

So please use this book as if it were your personal coaching session with me. I have designed it to take you on a journey of self-discovery and insightful learning. Be ready, because it's going to challenge some of your thinking and some of your beliefs. It's even going to make you rethink the way you do things, but it will provide you a roadmap for achieving the success that you've been eager to achieve in many areas of your life. Just remember, on this journey, only YOU can do the driving.

CHAPTER ONE:
Redefining Success

Now is the Time to Reassess

THERE COULDN'T BE A MORE APPROPRIATE TIME to consider reinventing yourself than right now. Think about the time in which we live. We're recovering from one of the worst global economic recessions since the Great Depression of the 1930s; major corporations have collapsed; people are being devastated by job loss, prolonged unemployment, home foreclosures, overwhelming debt, the loss of their entire life savings, and suffering with the highest rates of stress and depression that America has seen in decades.

In fact, according to statistics published by Mental Health America (mentalhealthamerica.net), depression now affects more than 21 million American children and adults annually; and it's the leading cause of disability in the United States for individuals ages 15 to 44. It's during difficult times such as these that domestic violence and child abuse rates rise, violent crimes soar, marriages fall apart, families are destroyed, and suicide rates increase. What's even more startling, according to a recent Boston Globe report, is that unemployed people are two to three more times likely to commit suicide—and the risk rises the longer someone remains without a job.

So, as a nation and as individuals, we are facing a crisis at the crossroads. It's in these times of unprecedented challenges, overwhelming change, and increasing complexities that we come face to face with the realities of life—and we have to make critical decisions. And the decisions we make right now in the midst of turmoil and transition may affect the rest of our lives.

Those who have lost their entire life savings are faced with making decisions about how they're going to recover some semblance of normalcy just to live day to day. Others who have lost their job and the income associated with it must make decisions as to what strategies they will utilize in order to vie with the more than 11 million Americans currently unemployed and competing for a job.

This crisis at the crossroads brings not only new challenges but, depending upon how you look at life's challenges, new opportunities, new possibilities, and new ways of looking at life and at yourself. First, this crisis represents an opportunity to redefine who you are, to think about why you exist, to examine what strengths and gifts and talents you possess, and to define your dreams. It's a time to ask yourself if you are where you want to be in life and, if not, to discover where you do want to be.

Second, now is the perfect time to reassess your priorities, your direction, and the path you've taken so far. It's a time to reflect on what you've done well and what's not worked well for you, to look at your life, both past and present, your actions, behaviors, and attitudes, and determine if they're helping you or hindering you on your path to success. And by so doing, you will determine not only what's possible but what you need to do differently.

And third, after you reassess where you are in life, it is necessary to reposition yourself for future success. This means laying out a plan complete with goals, strategies, resources, and time frames so that you can accomplish better results in your future than you have in your past.

Self-Assessment for Redefining Success

The following self-assessment questions are for you to reflect on in order to get you started on this journey of redefining success for your life. I use these questions for my own clients. I encourage you to engage in some deep thought and introspection; be as open and as honest with yourself as possible. I understand that you may be experiencing a crisis at the crossroads, but in order for you to take your life to the next level you must first start with yourself. Take whatever time you need to respond thoughtfully and honestly to each question. And if you don't have an immediate answer to a question, take the time to develop a meaningful response. **RYW**

1. How do you define success and what does it look like for you?
2. What do you value most in life and why?
3. Are you where you want to be in life, and if not, why?
4. What is your life motto?
5. How might you describe yourself? How would you summarize yourself in less than two sentences? Let's say, for instance, that you have to give your elevator speech (a brief description of who you are) and tell people not only who you are, but what you do, what you see as your life mission, and why they should care. How would you be able to say all that in less than two sentences?
6. What do you like least about your life?
7. Are you demonstrating the right actions, behaviors, and attitudes?
8. If not, what behavioral changes and attitude adjustments do you need to make?
9. What are you most proud of?
10. What mistakes do you keep repeating?
11. What lessons have you learned this past year? What lessons have you learned over the last five years?
12. Consider your closest relationships. Which of them are healthy for you? Which ones are actually toxic?
13. What priorities do you need to shift?

Remember: The *Reinvent Yourself Workbook* provides exercises, reflection questions, and personal assessments based on the material presented in this chapter. WHEN YOU SEE THIS SYMBOL **RYW**, IT MEANS THAT THERE IS A CORRESPONDING EXERCISE OR ACTIVITY FOR YOU TO COMPLETE. Working these exercises will help you to better integrate the material and focus your efforts towards reinventing yourself and achieving success in moving to the next level in your life. Visit **www.drshirleydavis.com/store**.

14. In conjunction with shifting priorities, what's on your plate that needs to come off? Because there are some priorities that you may move around and keep on your plate, but there are some things that you may need to take off your plate altogether.
15. What new skills do you need to learn?
16. What new goals have you set or will set this year?
17. What additional education do you need to obtain?
18. What new career path do you need to take? Or what business do you need to start?
19. What resources do you need to leverage? And who else do you need to bring into your network to achieve success?
20. What legacy do you want to leave behind?

Once you've had an opportunity to respond to these 20 questions and write down the personal reflections that they elicit from you, we will take them one by one and give them some more thought. Let's start with the first one, about redefining success, and refine what success means to you.

How Do You Define Success?

As we know, one's definition of success is going to vary from person to person, based on situations and circumstances. So it's important to know what success means to you in an effort to establish your life plans, your goals and strategies, and determine the resources and the time frames necessary for you to succeed. Knowing how you define success for yourself will help you measure your progress toward achieving it. It will help keep you focused and, more importantly, it will ward off some of the Negative Influences of Other People. (I call them the NIOPs)

The *Standard Dictionary* defines success as two things: First, the achievement of something desired, planned, or attempted. But the dictionary's second definition for success is the attainment of wealth, position, honors, status, or the like. Both of these definitions seem to have something missing for me. The first definition seems to be right, but it falls short, because it describes the positive outcome of a goal. Is that what success is all about? From my experience, achieving a goal can lead to a short-term success, but so many times that's merely a fleeting experience.

The second dictionary definition, attaining wealth and position and honor and status, gives us what society holds up as attaining success. But this definition in itself would leave out many humble and truly successful people who are not defined by their wealth or by a title or a position. These are people who have lived incredibly successful lives and left a legacy that even today we still embrace and celebrate—people such as soldiers, teachers, civil rights leaders, police officers, parents and grandparents, and many of our other unsung heroes.

So if success is not about achieving goals or wealth and power and status or fame, what is it about?

I have coached many professionals, at various levels and stages in their careers, and these have included entry-level and mid-level supervisors and managers, officers up to and including vice presidents, senior VPs, chiefs, and CEOs. And I often ask them how they define success in their lives. Consistently, their definitions have varied based on gender, age, ethnicity, and their stage in life. But there are some commonalities. Here are a few examples of some of the most common responses I hear.

Some say that success is about having a great job and making good money. Some say their fulfillment lies in their personal relationship with their spouse or their significant other and with their children. Some feel that success is being personally wealthy and being able to buy anything they want. It's having the car of their dreams. It's winning the lottery. Some even tell me that success is being spiritually grounded in their faith, having good health, and living a long life. For others, success is retiring and being able to travel around the world.

I'm sure that many of these definitions resonate with you, as they do with most Americans. Statistics confirm that 40 to 45 percent of Americans—that's nearly 100 million Americans—make New Year's Day resolutions and set goals under the premise that their lives will be better off and more successful if they accomplish these new goals. The most common New Year's resolutions include losing weight and getting healthier, finding a new job, spending more time with loved ones and friends, quitting smoking, and getting out of debt. Even so, according to a recent *USA Today* article, nearly 50 percent of those goals are abandoned by the end of January, and only 40 percent of them are maintained beyond six months.

Where Do You Invest Your Time, Talent, and Treasure?

One way I encourage my clients to consider how they define success is to have them look at how and where they invest their mental, emotional, financial, spiritual, and physical energy. If I were coaching you, I'd want to know what you really spend the majority of your time doing and thinking about, and planning for and working toward. If I looked at your daily planner and your checkbook, and at your debit and credit card statements, what would it tell me about what's most important to you?

I'm a big believer that where one invests one's time, talent, and treasure is a clear demonstration of where one's heart is committed. Where you commit your resources and energy says a lot about who you are and where you're going, where you've been and what you believe, and what legacy you will leave. One of my favorite authors, John Maxwell, has written a number of great books on success and leadership (*How Successful People Think; The Difference Maker; 21 Irrefutable Laws of Leadership*, to name a few). He describes success as a journey. It's like a cross-country trip—just use your imagination and envision such a trip with me. It's a trip that's filled with beautiful scenic views and signs and guideposts. But also along the way, the trip comes up against rocky roads, hills, valleys, mountains, and deserts. So in order to get to the right destination, you have to have a roadmap or a navigation system. Unfortunately, too many people take trips without using a roadmap and refuse even to ask for directions when they get lost.

The message is that success doesn't just happen. Like most things, it requires that you go through a process or a journey in order to achieve it. You may ultimately reach your destination, but along the way you will experience some peaks and some valleys. Successful people know this, and they're willing to take this journey.

Let's address a few more traits of successful people. They actively invest in themselves. They require constant self-discovery. They're growing and developing new knowledge, skills, attitudes, and perspectives. Plus, they're meeting new people and expanding their network, and doing things that benefit others as well as their society.

Unfortunately, most of us are not making the right investment of our time; we are not doing things that lead to success. Research tells us that the average American spends 20 to 28 hours a week—that's three to four hours a day!—watching television, when we could be using that time developing fresh skills or learning something new. *The Consumer Expenditure Report* published in 2011 by the Bureau of Labor Statistics revealed that individual consumers only spent $945 on education for the year. (This includes personal development activities such as attending a seminar/workshop, taking a college course, learning a new language, etc.) And purchasing reading materials made up only 0.2 percent of the average consumer's income, which equates to about $118 a year. This means the average consumer spent only $9.83 a month on reading materials—Yes, that's correct: only $9.83 a month!

More recently, a Huffington Post/YouGov poll conducted in October 2013 revealed that 28 percent of Americans haven't read a book in the past year. And, what's even more shocking, the *Consumer Expenditures Report for 2011* mentioned above revealed that the average consumer spent nearly $2,700 on entertainment, almost $500 on alcoholic beverages, $323 on tobacco products, $588 on personal care products, and over $1,800 on clothing.

Wow! I don't know about you, but the message is clear. If I were to look at the average American's bank statements and credit card bills and daily planners and see where they're investing most of their time and their money, I'd likely see time spent at the movies, video stores, concerts, shopping malls, liquor stores, restaurants, hair care product and nail salons, day spas, and other personal care shops. But I wouldn't see much time spent at the library or buying a book from the local bookstore, or attending a seminar at the local college, or even listening to motivational CDs or DVDs or MP3s—and I certainly wouldn't see time spent enrolling in a career or professional development program.

If you're one of those consumers who finds him or herself spending frivolously and wastefully without anything to show for it at the end of the year, or at the end of each month, now is the time to redefine what success means to you. Is success for you a repeat of that vicious cycle of dressing up outward appearances and having a short-lived good time on the weekend, only to wake up every day trying to fill a void and facing an emptiness caused by a lack of fulfillment? Do you want to enjoy life or endure life? Do you want success in every area of your life? Remember, success starts with oneself, and it works its way outward—not the opposite. And when you have true success, when you have true fulfillment, it flows through every area of your life.

The Four Common Traits of Successful People

Passion

Stephen Covey, who's another one of my favorite authors, wrote the book *The 8th Habit*. He's also the author of another best-selling book you may be familiar with, *The 7 Habits of Highly Effective People*. In *The 8th Habit*, he describes four common traits of successful people. First is passion, second is vision, third is discipline, and fourth is having a conscience. Covey describes passion as being the combined energy, drive, talent, will, and genuine desire necessary to accomplish something. That passion pushes you to go beyond what's expected of you and what's normal, and it will test your unlimited potential.

So, I ask you: Are you pursuing your passion? Are you doing something that really drives you? Are you excited about what you're doing? Do you have something that takes you to greater heights and makes you want to get up in the morning? Are you passionate about the work you're doing and the career you've chosen, or even the person you call your partner or your significant other? If you're not pursuing your passion, true fulfillment will remain a distant dream. **RYW**

Vision

The second trait he writes about is having a vision. A vision is really the blueprint for your life. It lays out what you're aiming to be or to become, or even to do in the future. It takes into account where you've been, where you are now, and what's possible. It's really a roadmap that guides and influences the choices and decisions you have to make on a daily basis.

William Blake, the famous 18th-century painter and poet, put it this way: "When people have no vision, development of the mind's capacity to create is neglected and they will fall prey to the human tendency towards victimization." His quote is still true and relevant today in the 21st century. **RYW**

Discipline

The third trait Stephen Covey writes about in *The 8th Habit* is discipline. If you plan to bring your vision into reality, it's necessary for you to be disciplined. It's important to have positive conditioning and control of your mind, your desires, your actions, beliefs, words, and even your habits. In order to obtain your goals, you must have the discipline to tackle or endure whatever it takes to succeed. This means that when things get tough, you get tougher. When things go south, you go north. You have to make sure that you've got friends who will stick with you, and if they should no longer stick with you, you stand your ground anyway. When you start to feel yourself losing hope and confidence, you keep pressing toward the prize, and you never give up. **RYW**

Conscience

The fourth trait Stephen Covey describes in *The 8ᵗʰ Habit* that successful people have in common is that they have a conscience. This means that they have the moral compass to distinguish between what is right and what is wrong. I know that this sounds pretty simple and that it really is relative, because people define right and wrong in their own worlds, based on their own situations, in the framework of their own beliefs. But having a conscience really is about driving us toward meaning and contribution; our conscience should act as the guidepost for our vision, our discipline, as well as our passion.

One of the most important traits that I've seen and observed in successful people is that they have a positive self-image and an extremely positive attitude. Self-image is very personal to me; it's something that I consider a very important attribute; I consider it a key and critical ingredient to being successful, whether in work or at home or in your community or in whatever you do, because self-image is the mental picture of how you see yourself. It's the tangible quality on the inside that you project to others. Maintaining a healthy self-image is important because if you don't have self-love and self-respect, you certainly won't treat others with that same love and respect. **RYW**

Self-Image Derailers

We have to love ourselves first before we can love our neighbor or anyone else; and it's my belief that everyone battles with some form of low self-image at some point in their life. And yes, so do the most attractive, the wealthiest, and the most privileged, powerful, and spiritual. We all deal with what I call self-image derailers.

Self-image derailers are those factors or issues that hinder us from being able to see beyond our own limitations—those factors that keep us living beneath our potential and prohibit us from achieving our greatness. Self-image derailers keep us from realizing our own capabilities—mental, physical, or emotional. In coaching my clients, whether it's the senior-level executive or the small-business owner, the entry-level worker or the college student, one of the most common things I find in our sessions is that they all are battling with one or more self-image derailers. Let me describe a few of them. **RYW**

Fear

One self-image derailer that I come across quite often is fear. People have a lot of fears right now, and it's understandable. We are living in very difficult and unprecedented times, and it causes people to experience great concerns and fears. Fear comes in a number of different forms. Some of the most common fears include the fear of taking risks, fear of the unknown, fear of failure, fear of dying, fear of heights, fear of closed spaces, fear of public speaking—and the fear of actually being successful! That's just for starters.

Because of fear, some people stay on jobs where they're miserable, but they are afraid to step out and take a chance. They may have great ideas—ideas that could impact someone else's life or impact the world around them, but they've talked themselves out of it because of fear. You could be an entrepreneur, start your own business, and be successful, but you're afraid that it will fail, that you will fail. You may dream of having a loving and committed relationship with the man or woman of your dreams, but you've resigned yourself to being alone because you fear that you're too old or too fat, or too this or too that, or you're afraid the next person will treat you like the last one did.

While fear is both a learned behavior and a part of human nature, oftentimes it's just a figment of our imagination, a negative anticipation or a suspicion of what might happen in the future. Sometimes, it's based on our own experiences from the past or on what we've heard from others and believed. Some spiritual leaders have defined fear as False Evidence Appearing Real (FEAR). Fear has also been described as being the opposite of faith.

Holding on to the Past

Another self-image derailer is holding on to the past. I can't tell you how many people and clients I've run into and coached over the past few years who are holding on to these kinds of issues—issues that are keeping them from achieving greatness and any level of success in their lives. They're holding on to past failures, past hurts, and even past relationships. So many people go through life holding on to these issues and harping on the past for years and years, and they never let them go. Rather than looking at failures as a learning experience and a growing opportunity, they see them as their downfall; or they see them as an excuse to stop trying; or as a reason to be critical and judgmental of other people; or even as a way to stay within their comfort zone. **RYW**

John Maxwell, that author I mentioned earlier in this chapter, also wrote a book called *Failing Forward* in which he tells us that it's OK to fail at something and to fall—we just need to "fall forward." This simply means that we need to learn from our failures, and learn from our mistakes, and not be afraid to get back up and take our lives to the next level because we learned from that mistake. Falling doesn't mean that you've reached the end of the road. You can use it as a springboard to the next level in your life.

The gospel artist Donnie McClurkin wrote a song called "We Fall Down, But We Get Up." His song resonated so much with so many people that it actually crossed over into the secular airwaves and has been played on radio stations around the world. The reason that song is so powerful is because of its message, that even though we make mistakes, it doesn't matter—we can get up. And there's a huge audience of people striving to get up.

One of my mentors used to say, "If you fall down and you can look up, you can get up." There's an opportunity for all of us to learn from our mistakes, because we all make them. No one is exempt from failing, from making mistakes, from having hiccups in their life. But the difference between those who succeed and those who stay stuck is that those who succeed realize that failing is a natural part of the journey toward success. **RYW**

Surrounding Yourself with NIOPs

The last self-image derailer I want to discuss is the one that I briefly touched upon earlier; and it's about being surrounded by what I call the NIOPS—the Negative Influences of Other People. And sometimes it's not the negative influence of other people; it's closer to home—it's our own continual negative self-talk.

Most of us have been surrounded by negativity and negative people much of our lives, starting at childhood. We may have experienced it at school with peer pressure or with those who teased or bullied us. We see it in newspaper headlines, on the Internet, and we hear it on the radio. We have witnessed the enormous number of negative events our country has suffered in the way of terrorist attacks, natural disasters, and epidemics. Even the recession that we're recovering from is perpetuating a lot of those negative feelings and continual negative self-talk.

Unfortunately, we even experience negative influences from those who are closest to us, such as our friends and our parents, even our spouses or significant others, who become naysayers and aren't supportive of our dreams. They might remind us of our past mistakes or bring up our failures or limitations. Obviously, those who are closest to us can sometimes hurt us the most, because they tend to hold on to things they know about us, even when we've moved on and moved past those things.

If you don't believe me, consider this scenario: You're in a relationship with someone; maybe it's your spouse or significant other. You go and share with a member of your family something that's happened between you, whether it's a bad argument or that you were cheated on or verbally abused—whatever it was. That family member oftentimes will never forget; it's hard for them to forgive, even if you and your significant other have reconciled and forgiven each other and started to move forward. Family members are often the ones who have the hardest time letting go.

So we have to be careful about that, because sometimes they are the ones who tell us that our dreams and goals are stupid, or they may make fun of our efforts to succeed. They may even tell us that we can't do something simply because of who our parents are or where we came from or, as I said, what they might know about us and our past. These are the NIOPs, the Negative Influences of Other People. These kinds of influences can shatter our self-esteem and our confidence and even our will to strive toward anything positive. **RYW**

We have to eliminate those voices of negative influence in our lives and replace them with voices of support and encouragement. In a later chapter, I'll discuss reevaluating relationships and exploring whether or not the people who are closest to you are helping you or hindering you on your way to achieving your success. I know, as I write about negative self-talk and being negative, that it's no wonder people tend to be negative more often than they are complimentary or talk about the positive things that happen in life. We have all complained and criticized and been negative at some point in our lives.

Constant Complaining

Consider how we deal with customers. Customer service statistics indicate that when people have a bad customer service experience they tell ten people. But when they have a really good experience they only tell one person. Why is that? Why is that we tend to focus more on the negative than we do on the positive? Why is that we tend to complain more than we compliment? I know we all expect good customer service, but when we do get service that goes above and beyond our expectations, why is that we don't tell that many people?

We do the same thing in our relationships, on our job, in our home, and with ourselves. We tend to focus on the negative aspects of a relationship and what the other person does wrong, versus the things that he or she may do right. On the job—think about it—we sometimes complain about our bad bosses or our crazy coworkers or some new policy we disagree with.

In particular, we tend to be really negative about ourselves. Think about this statistic: nearly 75 percent of women complain about their own personal appearance, and 85 percent of those women want to lose weight.

We're constantly focusing on our inabilities and our inadequacies and our weaknesses. It happens when we stand in front of the mirror and we're getting dressed. When is the last time you said to yourself, "Girl, you look good," or "Man, you are quite the handsome gentleman," or "I did an awesome job." When was the last time you admitted, "This product I created is great." "That was a wonderful idea." Oftentimes, we're doing the opposite; we're looking in the mirror and saying, "Boy, I'm too fat." "Boy, I can't stand my hair." "Man, I'm getting gray." "Man, I'm looking older and older." "I hate how this outfit makes me look." We make all kinds of comments like that; we're constantly looking at what's wrong with us and what's inadequate about us, instead of looking at the great attributes we have.

We still make statements like, "I'll never amount to much." "I can't do that." "I'll never be anything." Or, "I won't be able to achieve that because I'm too old (or too young or too uneducated)." "I'm a single parent." "I'm a woman." "I'm disabled." "I'm divorced." "I'm an ex-felon." We have a lot of crutches and a lot of excuses for why we can't get things done.

Moreover, psychologists estimate that over 80 percent of what we say to ourselves about ourselves is negative. That means that we spend much of our day thinking negative thoughts about who we are. If we believe that we're a loser or that we're weak or inferior, it will manifest in our attitude and in our actions. Our beliefs, whether true or false, have great power, and the words we speak to ourselves can give us life or they can destroy our dreams.

You Are Your Own Greatest Limitation

I believe that you have no limitations except the ones you have accepted from others and those that you have imposed on yourself. If you truly know why you were born, and how gifted and talented and valuable you are, then you have to believe that there's nothing you can't achieve—because you know your purpose. The problem is that most people don't know what their purpose is or even their potential or their capabilities. Most people haven't really explored their true passions or done the work to identify their true gifts and skills and strengths. They allow other people to define them; they allow other people to tell them what they should be doing and who they should become, and that's what's making them miserable—literally. **RYW**

I say to people all the time that when you don't know your purpose other people will define you; and when you allow other people to define you and tell you who you are and what you're created to do, you are allowing them to confine you. Research tells us that people who don't have a good self-image are more likely to have more health problems. They commit suicide more often; they tend to be poor performers at work; they're unable to enjoy healthy relationships; and they aren't good money managers. People with low self-esteem sometimes use food, shopping, drugs, drinking, or other unhealthy addictions and habits to fill a void. Some people will actually isolate themselves from friends and loved ones. All of these factors explain why not enough people ever achieve their true potential and why nearly 75 percent of Americans are content to live a life of mediocrity instead of excellence.

Summary

- Now is the perfect time to reassess your priorities, your direction, and the path you've taken so far; to reflect on what you've done well and what's not worked well for you; to look at your life, both past and present, your actions, behaviors, and attitudes, and determine if they're helping you or hindering you on your path to success.

- Only you can do what it takes for you to succeed. Only you can define what success means for you; it doesn't come from others. So if success is not about achieving goals or wealth and power and status or fame, what is it about for you?

- According to Stephen Covey, there are four common traits of successful people: passion, vision, discipline, and conscience. I added a fifth trait: a positive self-image and an extremely positive attitude.

- We all fail, but that doesn't make us a failure. Learn to fail forward.

There are four ways to derail your self-image: fear, holding on to the past, the negative influences of other people, and constant complaining.

- Don't be your biggest limitation. Get out of your own way and learn to affirm yourself.

CHAPTER TWO:
Reassessing Your Purpose and Your Vision

Finding the Answers

I'VE LAID THE GROUNDWORK by helping you to redefine what success means to you. The next step in the journey of reinventing yourself is to determine your purpose and your vision. "Who am I?" "Why am I here?" "Why do I exist?" "What is my purpose?" These are some of the most basic questions in life. I alluded to this in chapter one. When you start answering these questions, you'll bring new meaning to every aspect of your life—to your career, to your relationships, and even to your responses to life's challenges.

Many people spend years trying to find their purpose, and yet so few of them are living a life of fulfillment and meaning. I've said for several years that many people die at the age of 30 but they don't get buried until they're 80; and that's because so many people go through life without meaning. They're empty, they have a void, and they're searching for significance and a clear vision for their lives. They go through life trying to find direction, and by the time they get older they've got more regrets than they can resolve.

It's been said that the poorest person in the world is the person without a dream. But I would say that the most frustrated person in the world is the person who has a dream that never becomes a reality. Do you know where the richest place on earth is? In my opinion, the richest place in the world is not the gold mines in Ghana or the diamond mines in Africa—I've been there and they are absolutely beautiful; you'll see some of the most fascinating gems in the world. It's not even the rich oil lands of Saudi Arabia or Mexico. I think the richest place on earth is the cemetery, because in the cemetery lie many dreams that were never attained; life-changing and motivating songs that were never sung; cures to cancer and other diseases that were never discovered; Nobel Peace Prize winners who were never known; even best-selling authors who were never published. The list is endless. We all have dreams—dreams of visual manifestations of our purpose, and their seeds of destiny planted in our hearts.

Others May See Your Purpose Before You Do

Your purpose is probably something that you enjoyed and discovered when you were at a young age. It's something that continues to follow you from that young age even into your adulthood. I knew at a young age that I was gifted to speak, to be a leader, and that I had a passion to help and to teach others. My mom tells me that my kindergarten teacher saw that gift of speaking and asked her one day when I was about five or six years old to be a speaker at my kindergarten graduation ceremony. Of course, I don't remember this story from that far back, but I do know that through a series of events in my life I was constantly being put in front of groups to speak, mostly by teachers who recognized that I had that kind of a gift. Although I received good grades in school, I was always talkative. So on my progress reports I'd have all these A's and B's, but then under the section where it listed opportunities for improvement and the teachers could write in their comments, they would write: "Shirley is a great student, and very smart, but she needs to focus on being less talkative in class."

I remember this pattern of evaluations followed me throughout grade school and all the way to high school. My favorite classes were English and writing composition, speech and drama, and communications. I remember having a knack for connecting with people. I was never short on words. I enjoyed public speaking and writing and was never afraid to do that. In fact, I would write short stories and poems just as a hobby. Then I began developing messages out of my own experiences and writing them down. Soon it became clear to me that my purpose was to train, coach, teach, and empower others with knowledge, strategies, and skills, and to enable them to see a larger vision for themselves so that they could find meaning, fulfillment and success in every area of their life.

So it's not a surprise that I am writing about reinventing oneself and how to have success in every area of our life. It's something that I was doing long before I took on the formal title of success coach. For years I was an advisor, a mentor, and a manager; and I liked to help people grow and develop new skills. I got excited and felt fulfilled when I would see people have "Ah ha!" moments and epiphanies from something that I shared with them or coached them through.

Recognize Your Gifts and Talents

As I recognized my own purpose and calling and gifts and talents through a series of events in my life, I also started falling into certain things—certain jobs, certain career paths, educational pursuits, and opportunities. All those things helped me to grow, and to build and develop my skills and my talents. Like me, we all have some natural gifts and talents, but we also have to grow, develop, perfect, and master them so that they become effective; and when we use them properly and purposefully, they are a blessing to other people.

As I embraced my purpose in life, and I realized what I was really called to do, I discovered that I liked it. And to some degree, that enjoyment showed up in every facet of my life. For example, in my career, I found that I was drawn to jobs that needed my talents and skills in speaking, writing, leadership, and working with people. Then I became very good at it and I started doing a couple of things. First, I recognized the gift, so I wrote it down. And this is the first thing I would encourage you to do: Recognize and identify that you do have a gift and a talent—as we all do—and write down what that gift or that talent is. You may want to go back and revisit the 20 questions I presented in the first chapter. Write down your answers if you haven't already. Read them again and give them some more thought.

Sometimes, you may not know what your specific skill or talent is. Sometimes, the realization may come to you through other people because they recognize it in you first. In my case, it was my kindergarten teacher and my parents who first saw that gift in me when I was a little girl.

Develop Your Gift

The second step then is to begin developing your gift and working on it. Work on it over time, develop it over time, and pay attention to how it is growing. You start by preparing the gift; then you start perfecting it; and ultimately you become a master at it. Not only did my teacher and my grandparents recognize my gift, they began helping me to nurture and develop it over time by exposing me to different opportunities, coaching me along the way, and reaffirming me. This is why it is so important to have people around you who will see things in you that you may not see yourself; people who will bring out the best in you; and who will push you to do more than you think is possible. It may not be your parents, or your teacher. It may be a co-worker, a good friend, a spiritual leader, a client or a customer. Who is that person in your life? If you don't have people like that around you, I encourage you to find them. We'll cover this topic more in Chapter 6.

Embrace Your Gift

The third thing you must do when you discover your specific gift and talent is to fully embrace it and recognize that you are good at it. Embrace your gift as a part of your purpose and as a part of your destiny. This means that your gift becomes a part of who you are. It becomes a habit. It becomes your nature. The last thing about your gift—now that you're clear what it is, you've started to perfect it, grow it, and develop it over time—is to start to utilize that gift and give it away. This is the means to accomplishing your purpose in life and being effective both at your journey toward success and in helping others along the way. The gifts that we have are not just for us. Our gifts and our talents and our purpose are all about helping other people. It's about leaving behind a legacy; it's about making the world a better place as a result of you being here. That's why we were created. When we know our purpose, when we're walking in our purpose, when we're working it, developing it, and giving it away, we are on our journey toward achieving success.

Let me restate this. When you start understanding your gift and you start walking in it and you start utilizing it and being a blessing to others, it's a fulfilling thing. When you see the impact that your gift has on other people and you see the value and the influence that it has (and you have) to change the world around you, it really starts to energize you, it drives you, and becomes your life's ambition. **RYW**

Help Your Children Discover Their Purpose

I have a 19-year-old daughter. She'll be turning 20 in a few months and becoming a junior in college in the fall. I can remember that she had a calling to sing at a young age. She was gifted at it. At the age of two and a half, she sang her first solo. She was in a small daycare and they were putting on a program at the end of the year to close out that particular school year. Her teacher asked her to sing a solo. She took it on willingly and was very excited to be able to do it. She had not grasped the enormity of appearing before a crowd. Like most Americans, this is our greatest fear—public speaking. But as a child, she had not learned that fear yet. She grabbed the microphone and she

Remember: The *Reinvent Yourself Workbook* provides exercises, reflection questions, and personal assessments based on the material presented in this chapter. WHEN YOU SEE THIS SYMBOL **RYW**, IT MEANS THAT THERE IS A CORRESPONDING EXERCISE OR ACTIVITY FOR YOU TO COMPLETE. Working these exercises will help you to better integrate the material and focus your efforts towards reinventing yourself and achieving success in moving to the next level in your life. Visit **www.drshirleydavis.com/store**.

sang with all of her might. She exuded such confidence and passion, although she was loud and strong and flat and out of tune, but you could see that she was very comfortable singing; she enjoyed it. As a parent, obviously, I was proud; but I also recognized that she had a gift to sing and wasn't afraid to do it in front of people. She had a voice, even though she was a little bit flat, but at two-and-a-half years old how can we expect her to sing like Whitney Houston or Aretha Franklin?

So I encouraged her over the years to join choirs, to take voice and music lessons, and to take part in school programs. I also allowed her to participate in church youth programs and performances, and I began to see her develop and grow. Now, at the age of 19, my daughter is singing at different events around the country, and even around the world. She's performed at state and local events, at graduations and birthday parties, and at all kinds of anniversary celebrations. I've taken her with me to youth retreats and conventions and conferences around the world, and I've even had her open for me before I deliver a keynote speech.

One of the things I'm most proud of is that she competed in her first pageant competition in 2011 and won. It was the local Miss America Scholarship Pageant for Maryland. She had seen me compete, coach, and judge pageants since she was in Pampers, but she never expressed an interest. I was not one of those parents who wanted to live vicariously through my child's life, so I never pushed her to compete. But one day out of the blue, she expressed an interest in trying out for the Miss Montgomery County Outstanding Teen Pageant. Of course, I was ecstatic, and I jumped at the opportunity to prepare and coach her for success.

The pageant had a talent competition and she knew exactly what hers would be. That night, after months of preparation and practice, she walked out onto the stage. She couldn't have been more beautiful, poised, and ready. Unlike her first performance at the age of two and a half at that small daycare some 14 years earlier, this time when she opened her mouth to sing, it gave you chills. She sang "Circle of Life" from "The Lion King," and this time she wasn't flat and she wasn't off key—and she still wasn't fearful. She was awesome, and the judges agreed. She was crowned Miss Montgomery County's Outstanding Teen 2011. Her first pageant, her first serious competition, and she won—the first teen of color to hold that title. Her gift had opened a new door of opportunity because she recognized it at a young age; she developed it and mastered it over time; and she allowed it to work for her.

Over the years, I've seen her voice develop and grow. Now she has range, she understands pitch, and she's writing her own songs. Just last year she went into the studio with the songs she wrote. She coproduced the songs for her first CD project; she sang all of them beautifully; and they really showcase her giftedness in music.

She knows very clearly that she has a gift to sing and perform. When people would ask her at five and six years old what she wanted to do when she grew up, her response without any hesitation was "I want to be seen and heard." As a teen, she tweaked it a bit so she can now articulate that she wants to be an "international entertainer and philanthropist." And today, that is what she's doing. She's pursuing a Communications and Public Relations degree in college, while still studying, writing, and making music.

Mentor Your Children

It's so important as parents, mentors, and as guardians that we help our children and other young people to discover their purpose. They all have talents; they all have interests and even passions; and we have to help tap into that and help them begin to grow and develop those gifts and talents at a very young age. We need to train them in the way they should develop, give them exposure, give them opportunities, and give them the support they need in order to hone and to develop their skills.

I also believe that even the people we have around us, those who are closest to us, have an opportunity to help identify our children's gifts and talents, to be that support network, and to be that voice of encouragement—to help them see their purpose, and why they exist, and how they can be a blessing to the world.

You Must Have a WHAT and a WHY

When you know your "what" and your "why," your "how" will take care of itself. Too many people are pursuing their "how"—how to do this, how to take this step, and how to take ten steps, and they don't understand "why" they're doing what they're doing. So, to really know your purpose, you have to have a "what"— what I'm supposed to be doing; you have to have a "why"—why I am doing this, and then your "how" will follow. Your how will fall into place. Until you find this kind of meaning, you'll live a life of frustration, bitterness, and emptiness, and you'll go through life trying to fill a void that cannot be satisfied. You may even try to fill that void with addictions, obsessions, impulses, and other unhealthy and hurtful habits. You will not find satisfaction until you find that thing that motivates, drives, and fulfills you.

Having the Right People Around You is Critical

If you want to understand your purpose, you can't just ask anybody. It's critical that you have the right people around you in your inner circle; these are the people who are the voices of influence in your life. You've got to go to the creator first, to the manufacturer, because you are a specific being. Someone created you. It's analogous to a product that you buy from a manufacturer. A manufacturer's warranty comes with that product, but there's also a specific way that that product is supposed to operate.

I recently bought one of my dream cars. (I have another dream car that I'll have to get a few years from now.) I bought a BMW; and it has a lot of bells and whistles, and a lot of features and options. Of course, I've mastered some of the basic things, like how to drive the car and put it in reverse and park; and I understand now where the locks are. These are just some of the basic features, but there's so much more to the car. In fact, I had to make an appointment with the BMW dealer to go and sit down for an hour or so with a technician who walked me through the specific options and features—so I could fully maximize my use of that car. Basically, I had to go back to the manufacturer. **RYW**

As we look at this from the perspective of who we are and why we were created, it's important that we go back to our Creator to understand what skills and gifts and talents we really have, why we were wired the way the we were, and what is our purpose. This is a critical step, because when you don't know the purpose of a thing, it's inevitable that you will abuse or misuse it. There's something in each of us that we were created to do. We were born to this specific generation, to this specific time. It's our responsibility to not take what we're supposed to do to the cemetery, to not take it to the grave, but to leave it as a legacy in the time we're allotted here on earth. The world should be a better place because we were here. So what will you leave behind as a result of your being here?

Your Purpose is the Life Story You Are Writing Every Day

Think about your epitaph or your obituary. What will people read about you when you've gone to your next life? What do you want people to say about the life you lived? What kind of legacy do you want to be known for?

I delivered a speech a few years ago called "This is Your Life." I asked the audience a very similar question: "What legacy will you leave behind?" And I asked them: "If you had to name a book that would be written about your life story after you were gone, what would the title of your book be? Would it be a mystery book or a suspense novel because you had no idea who you were, where you were going, or how you were going to get there? Did you keep everybody guessing about who you really were and what lay behind the exterior because you never trusted anyone enough to let them in? Or would your life story be a horror story or a thriller, because you lived your life in constant terror and dread, afraid of people or afraid of something, or because you terrorized others' lives and left them living tormented and afraid of you or fearful of life in general?"

I went on to ask: "Would your life be a drama, because you always stirred things up and loved lots of drama going on in your life? Would it be a comedy, because you found humor in life and discovered ways to laugh and have a good time and enjoy life's beauty, even in the face of challenge? Or conversely, would it be a comedy because you didn't take your life seriously and that your life was just a big joke?" And finally, I asked them: "Would your life be a love story, because you loved yourself, you gave of yourself to others, and you epitomized what it meant to make this world a better place because you were here?"

Every day we write the pages and the chapters of our life story. Our life story culminates in the legacy that we will leave behind. While we don't have control over when it's our turn to leave this earth, we do have control over how we choose to live our lives right here, right now. "Choose" is the operative word here. We have the power to choose the future. We have the power to choose our destiny. We can't do anything about the past; we only have the present and hopefully the future. Tomorrow is not promised to anybody and no one knows when their life will end, but what we can hope for is a better tomorrow based on the choices that we make right now. **RYW**

Start Building Today the Future You Want Tomorrow

Start today making a different choice that will propel you forward and not hold you back. In your pursuit of living a life of purpose, and as you move along your journey toward achieving success, you'll encounter obstacles and adversities and all kinds of brick walls along the way, but don't let people talk you out of your dream. Don't be paralyzed by fear or by failure. Fear and failure are a part of life. Life happens. We've all experienced failure, made mistakes, and faced trials and tests. Some are unexpected and others are anticipated, but we experience failure and make mistakes whether we're good people or bad people.

You've heard the saying, "Sometimes bad things happen to good people." Well, sometimes good things happen for bad people, but either way success does not always come easy and is not going to just fall into your lap. You've got to work for it. You've got to fight for it. You've got to be willing to put in long hours and then extra energy. You must be willing to sacrifice for it because anything worth having is worth fighting for. And you've got to decide how bad you want your dream to come true. How hungry are you to get it done? What are you willing to give up in order to achieve it?

Adversity Comes When You're Pursuing Your Purpose

When I was in my early 20s, and I figured out what I was born to do, I started pursuing it with passion. And it seemed like all hell started to break loose in my life the minute I started down that road toward getting it done. Everything seemed to rise up against me. I faced every kind of obstacle. All these adversities tried to discourage me and distract me and destroy me, and yet this is what happens to everybody. You figure out what you want to do; you start down the path toward something positive; and, as soon as you start pursuing it, obstacles surround you. Fear rears its ugly head. Friends betray you. Your finances become shaky.

In my life, the obstacles I faced came up against me in the form of divorce, financial hardships, the challenges of single parenting, the death of loved ones, toxic relationships, near-death experiences, friends who turned their backs on me, career setbacks—I can go on and on. I am sure that these challenges are very similar to the kinds you've faced, because we all face them.

Life Lessons for Dealing With Obstacles

Lesson 1:

Through all of these obstacles and challenges, I learned several life lessons about tests and trials. Let me share a few with you here. (I'll share others in subsequent chapters.) The first lesson I learned is that when life smacks you in the face, don't get bitter—get better! That's so important because people often hold on to bitterness until it stops and immobilizes them, and sometimes even paralyzes them from moving forward. You've got to get better, not bitter. You don't want to hold on to things for years and years, because usually it hinders you and not the other person you're holding it against. Quite frankly, sometimes other people don't even know the things we're holding against them; they don't know and they're in no way miserable because of it; we're the ones who are miserable.

Lesson 2:

The second lesson I learned is that even though you may have suffered a setback emotionally, financially, or even physically, you can still reinvent yourself. You don't have to allow your past to define your future. You can learn from your mistakes. You can make a decision not to repeat them, and to do better. As I always say, you have to admit your mistakes; you need to quit making them; and then you need to move forward and move past them. Admit it; quit it; and forget it.

That's the blessing in experiencing failures and making mistakes: Even though you fail, you're not a failure; and even though you've made a mistake, you are not the mistake. Through determination, willpower, and walking in your purpose, you can get back up and keep going. That's true success. No one who is successful will ever tell you that they've never had any setbacks or that they never had any failures. In fact, most successful people have become successful because they failed more times than they succeeded—and they learned how to learn from those mistakes.

Lesson 3:

The third lesson I learned is that you don't have to live as a victim. Just because someone hurt you deeply and left the scars to prove it, it doesn't make you a victim—it makes you a survivor. How you choose to characterize it and how you choose to look at it all depends on you. I choose to claim victory. If I didn't die in the test, and I've still got my sanity, and I'm still breathing, that makes me a survivor—and a victor. You may lose some battles, but you can ultimately win the war.

Sometimes we lose the battle with our finances by filing for bankruptcy or losing our home to foreclosure. Sometimes we lose the battle with our relationships by suffering a heart-wrenching divorce. Sometimes we lose the battle with our jobs by getting laid off or fired. But we can recover from all these setbacks. We can recommit to our purpose and we can reestablish our goals and our action plan; we can reposition and reinvent ourselves so that we get back on track and live out the purpose we are meant to live. We can regain our peace of mind, our sense of self-worth, our personal joy and meaning, and our spiritual foundation, which is our faith—these are all ingredients that will help us keep fighting the good fight until we finish our course.

Lesson 4:

The fourth lesson I learned about adversity is that if I don't learn from my past I'll continue to repeat those same mistakes. This is the definition of insanity: continuing to do the same thing over and over again and expecting different results. In school, if we take a test or an exam and we fail it, guess what? We have to retake it. And if we continue to fail the test we have to repeat the class. Tests are designed to assess our knowledge and ascertain whether or not we've learned the lesson. That's also what life's tests do for us: They present themselves to allow us to demonstrate that we've acquired knowledge and information. If we fail, we keep experiencing that same test. If we pass, we get to advance to the next level or to the next chapter in our lives. God forbid that you continue to take the same test over and over again, never learning, never applying knowledge, and never matriculating to the next level. You'll wake up one day 20 years later and realize your life has passed you by. **RYW**

Strategies to Avoid Failing

Preparation, Practice, Perserverance

No one likes failing tests, but there are some strategies to avoid failing—they are: preparation, practice, and perseverance. We've got to prepare for the test, understand what information we need to know. Then we have to practice and go through it, whether by regurgitating it to ourselves, having someone else help us practice, or by applying ourselves and getting hands-on experience. The perseverance piece is simply never giving up, learning from it, and continuing to apply yourself until you get to that place where you understand it. That goes back to the discipline that we were talking about earlier.

One other important point I want to make about preparation: My mentor used to say to me that it's better to be prepared and never have an opportunity than to have an opportunity and not be prepared. Think about that. You never know when your opportunity is going to come knocking, so you always have to be preparing as if that knock could come at any time. Preparation is all about living a life of expectation: You're expecting that knock to come, but you don't know when.

There have been times in my life when things have crossed my path and taken me by surprise. Even though they caught me off guard, I was prepared; but I was afraid to take a chance, and I second-guessed myself. I would say: "Oh, I'll get a second chance," or "I'll get better, and I'll get ready for it the next time." But I had a lot of regrets later because some of those opportunities never knocked again. Those experiences taught me to begin to expect the unexpected. When I figured out what I was supposed to be doing and made the proper preparations, I started pursuing my dreams and my passions with boldness and courage. I began to look for those opportunities and I was confident about them—and I was ready.

Jump First and Grow Your Wings on the Way Down

Most people are afraid to step out and pursue their dreams. They really haven't properly prepared. They're afraid that something's going to go wrong and that they haven't thought it through. Sometimes, however, when you've done all that you can do to prepare, you have to jump first and grow your wings on the way down. My mentor also used to tell me that: "Shirley, jump first and grow your wings on the way down." And I didn't understand what he meant at first, but he meant: "Shirley, you're prepared; your development is complete; you've been through all the courses; you've attended the conferences; I've been your coach for years; you've got the knowledge; you've got the confidence—Now it's time for you to get out there and do it." That meant a lot to me because what I realized in that one statement is that I couldn't keep waiting and waiting for my wings to grow and expand. I had to make sure that I got out there now that I was prepared. I had to go do something; I had to act. I couldn't keep sitting around waiting for the door of opportunity to knock; I had to go out there and pursue my dreams myself.

So, are you going to sit there for the rest of your life and be prepared and never do anything, never accomplish anything? I encourage you the same way my mentor encouraged me: You jump first and you grow your wings on the way down. That's important because as you have started to identify your skills and your purpose, what you were created to do, you're going to start to grow and develop, to nurture that gift and practice that skill. What you need to do more than anything is to start putting it into practice.

The key elements of success are preparation, practice, and perseverance. So don't run from failing. Don't run from making mistakes. Don't even run from the tests, because winners never quit and quitters never win. If at first you don't succeed, then join the success club. Thomas Edison failed more than a thousand times before inventing the light bulb. When the media asked him about it, Edison allegedly said: "I have not failed a thousand times; I have successfully discovered a thousand ways not to make a light bulb." Abraham Lincoln lost every election he ever ran except the presidency. Michael Jordan, who is considered one of the greatest athletes of all times, was cut from his high school varsity basketball team in the tenth grade.

There are three kinds of people in this world: those who make things happen, those who watch things happen, and those who wonder what happened. Which one of them are you? I hope that you're the kind of person who makes things happen, because in order to achieve anything in life, in order to really excel at your purpose, you've got to be the person who makes things happen, because success is not going to fall in your lap. You've got to go out and pursue it and make it happen. **RYW**

Vision is Different Than Purpose

I have mostly addressed purpose, so I now want to address vision. This chapter is entitled "Reassessing Your Purpose *and Your Vision.*" People often get these mixed up and use them interchangeably. They do work hand in hand, so let's take a close look at vision. But even before that, I want to focus on mission and mission statements.

I coach my clients that they need to have a statement of purpose, a brief statement describing why they exist. And I offer you the same advice. You need to have a mission statement to describe how you're going to accomplish your purpose; and then you need a vision statement to put into words where you're going. So what would that look like?

Think of the mission statement as being the how; the mission statement describes the methods and the strategies and the techniques you're going to use. You have your purpose, but now you have to further define it for your life. For example, your purpose might be that you want to become a doctor and save lives, but you want to take it a little bit further. You start by identifying in more detail how you're going to get there: You want to focus on women, so it may mean you want to be an obstetrician or a gynecologist. Or you want to focus on children, so you want to become a pediatrician. Or maybe you want to be a heart surgeon and so you specialize in cardiology.

You have defined your purpose, and in your mission statement you express in broad terms how you are targeting that purpose to help you accomplish it. This statement describes what makes you unique and different, what will cause you to stand out and do something that only you can do. **RYW**

That's the mission piece; the vision statement answers the "where" question—not so much where you are right now but where are you going and who you are becoming. The vision is an ideal picture in your mind about what your purpose should look like. Your vision is when you see your purpose in your mind and begin to imagine it. It's the ability to see farther than your physical eyes can see—to see not just what is, but what can be and how you can make it a reality.

Vision is also seeing the future before it comes into being; it's having a mental picture of your destiny. Organizations create vision statements all the time; usually it's a picture of what that organization wants to be three to five years out. You've got to do the same thing and create your vision in a more personal way. Vision is a primary motivator for human action and human behavior, and everything that we do should be because of the vision we have in our hearts.

Without vision people stumble all over themselves; without vision life has no meaning or sense of direction and activity is meaningless; without vision time has no purpose and resources have no application. Vision is the prerequisite for passion and the source of persistence. When you have vision, you know how to stay in the race and to complete the course.

As you think about your purpose, it's important that you also think about how you're going to achieve your purpose and what your future is going to look like. What does your vision tell you about your future three, five, ten, and twenty years from now? Your vision is the image that guides your success, and it's formed in terms of your contribution to society. As I addressed before, it's important that we think about our legacy—what do we want to leave behind? What do we want to be known for when we leave this earth? How much impact do we want to have as a result of our being here? The world should be a better place because we existed. **RYW**

In Conclusion

As I close this chapter, I can't emphasize enough how important it is not only to have a clear purpose but to understand your mission (your how) and your vision (your where). That clear vision helps to empower your purpose. It reveals the desire, the end result, and it provides the motivation for you to work toward the goal. That clear vision gives meaning to your mission. It gives you a target to aim for, and it helps you to see that target clearly. A vision is an ideal, but it's not impossible. It's a goal, but it's not unattainable. You will never be greater than the vision that guides you. That vision will require you to stretch your expectations, your aspirations, and your performance. Without that powerful, attractive vision, why even bother?

I say, "Watch and learn and wait." Even though we're all dealing with our own issues, everyone we meet has something to teach us. I have this rule that I call the three foot rule. If I come within three feet of someone else or if they come within three feet of me, there's either something they have for me or there's a blessing or something I have to give to them. That's why it's imperative that we create our own measure of success and then develop a personal strategy to achieve it. And be careful not to confuse your purpose in life with your personal goals. Although goals are crucial to achieving any kind of success, left alone they can become empty and lack direction.

You may set a hundred goals in your lifetime, but there is only one true purpose in life and that purpose should be the underlying core that gives your goals direction and meaning. When you understand your purpose, you understand that when people come into your life or cross your path, you're able to discern if it's for a reason, a season, or a lifetime.

Remember, all our dreams can come true if we have the courage to pursue them. No one is more important or worthy or even more special than you are. You have talents that no one else can offer. There is a special goodness and love inside of you. We have been fearfully and wonderfully made, and our creator made no mistakes when he made us. He knew exactly what he was doing. So never treat your own emotional, mental, physical, or even your spiritual health and well-being as an afterthought, because he didn't do that. Instead, make your own well-being a priority in your life because it is truly you that makes the difference. When you understand your purpose, you can leave this world better than when you entered it, and you can leave a legacy that continues to make an impact after you're gone. **RYW**

Summary

- Your purpose is likely something you enjoyed and discovered at a young age and has followed you into your adulthood.
- Once you recognize your purpose and calling, your gifts and talents, then you begin developing your gift and working on it; you embrace it and recognize that it is part of your purpose and your destiny.
- As parents, mentors, and guardians, help your children and other young people to discover their purpose, develop their talents, and follow their interests and passions by giving them exposure, opportunities, and support.
- Your purpose is your life story being written every day. Will it be a mystery or suspense story, a horror story or thriller, a drama or a comedy, a love story or an inspirational tale?
- There are four things to learn from adversity: Don't get bitter, get better; don't let your past define your future; you don't have to live as a victim; and it's by learning from mistakes that you grow.
- There is a strategy to avoid failing: it's called called preparation, practice, and perseverance.
- You need to have a mission statement to describe how you're going to accomplish your purpose and a vision statement to put into words where you're going.
- Your dreams can come true if you have the courage to pursue them.

CHAPTER THREE:
Reprioritizing Your Goals

Reflect on Your Year

IF YOU'RE LIKE ME, and like many Americans, life is hectic. If you're working a job, parenting, managing a relationship, taking part in activities or hobbies, or pursuing a specific interest, life is hectic. Even if you have friends and family commitments and you're out and about just living day to day, life is hectic. For me, every year around the November and December holiday season, I start to reflect on my life, but I do it because I start to feel drained and overwhelmed from a hectic and demanding travel and speaking schedule.

In the last chapter, I addressed purpose and vision and how important it is to start thinking about your future every day. You have to plan and identify where you're going, how you're going to get there, and what it's going to look like once you get there—in other words, what does success look like? You have to continue to plan ahead, even when you're living a demanding life and are responsible for so many things on a day-to-day basis. All of our plates are full, yet sometimes we have to just sit down, reflect on the day, on the month, and on the year, and reprioritize. When I sit down at the end of the year, I look back over the year to identify what has gone well in every area of my life. I try to identify specific things I have learned, mistakes or missteps that I have made, relationships I have been blessed or honored to have this past year—even those that came and went. It's an opportunity to sit back and reflect on where I need to go next—and this is the important piece around setting goals.

I make my living in the global talent management/human resources field, and I have an opportunity to travel around the world speaking to different organizations at different conferences and with various business leaders. I must have logged more than 20,000 miles last year by air, train, and ground transportation; and I spoke at more than 50 events around the world. What I didn't realize was that I was so busy, and I was out and about so much, that when the end of the year came around, I realized that I had not taken as much time out for myself to smell the roses, to pamper myself, to do some personal reflection, and to have some quiet time. I'm sure I've shaken more than 5,000 hands and received over 1,000 business cards—and given out double that many of my own. I'm very adept at social media; I'm constantly on LinkedIn, Twitter, and on Facebook. I make a lot of social media connections, and I'm constantly entertaining phone calls from colleagues, doing media interviews, and coaching people wanting advice and counsel about their career, or from HR professionals just wanting to get information on best practices, trends, and what I'm hearing about the changing global workforce. By November, I'm usually mentally, physically and even somewhat emotionally drained.

So, as we set goals for ourselves, it's important that we think about all these areas—whether it's our personal commitments, at home, in our relationships, in our volunteer and community service work, or in the social events that we attend. At some point, we have to make sure that we are taking care of ourselves, staying on the right path, and learning the right things. And we have to ask ourselves what impact we are making on the lives of those with whom we come in contact. At the end of the day, this is what our purpose and vision is all about. As we set

Remember: The *Reinvent Yourself Workbook* provides exercises, reflection questions, and personal assessments based on the material presented in this chapter. WHEN YOU SEE THIS SYMBOL **RYW**, IT MEANS THAT THERE IS A CORRESPONDING EXERCISE OR ACTIVITY FOR YOU TO COMPLETE. Working these exercises will help you to better integrate the material and focus your efforts towards reinventing yourself and achieving success in moving to the next level in your life. Visit **www.drshirleydavis.com/store**.

goals, we've got to make sure that, despite all that's on our plate, we are prioritizing and staying on track, staying focused, and making sure that we're disciplined and directed toward accomplishing our purpose and our mission in life.

A Change of Venue Is a Good Idea When Setting Life Plans

I've developed an annual ritual, and I've done it for at least the last seven years, of just getting away to a tranquil, quiet place where I can think and reflect. I review my successes and accomplishments for the year just ending. I look at setbacks I've experienced and mistakes and missteps I've made. And I figure out what I need to do differently to reprioritize, revise, or just reinvent myself. Whatever time works for you, I recommend that you just get away and do it. I do it at the end of the year because the first part of the New Year is approaching and it's the best time to be thinking about making a new start. I try to identify those things that I need to put into place so that I have the rest of the year to make those things happen. And I certainly don't want to repeat the same mistakes of the previous year, so it's important to inventory what worked and what didn't.

For me, it means getting away from home. I recommend you do that too because, if you're like me, being at home it's too easy to look around and see everything that needs to be done. It's so easy to get interrupted with phone calls when you're in your own house. If you've got children at home as well, obviously, you're not going to have a whole lot of peace and quiet. There are just too many distracters. So it's good to get away— even if you have to limit it to a day or two. It might be an overnight trip; it might be to a friend's house where you know that it's going to be a quiet place where you can get away. More often than not, friends will respect and appreciate your need for quiet and allow you that time. So that's the first step. **RYW**

Five Areas in Which to Plan and Set Goals

As I think about the coming year, I like to think about what I want to accomplish—again, aligning it with my purpose, vision, and mission for my life—and I look at five major categories of goals. I have looked at these five categories for the past seven or eight years. I encourage you to look at the same areas of your life and see how you can take specific steps to make them happen.

Health and Wellness Goals

Those areas in which I set goals include my personal goals, what I consider "me" goals. They include my health and wellness goals, my spiritual, family and household goals, and my financial goals. Health and wellness goals might include things like: "I'm going to make sure that I go the doctor at least twice a year for the purpose of having a preventative checkup." Let's say your goal is about controlling your weight. Most of the time, Americans set goals like this at the beginning of the year. Your goal could be losing weight or just watching your weight so that you neither gain nor lose any extra pounds. So you commit to watching what you eat; making sure that you are eating healthy; eating more vegetables; eating more fruits; drinking more water or juice or whatever works best. Whatever your personal goal, you have to make sure that you target how are you going to take better care of you. If you're dealing with a sickness or a certain illness, how are you going to do better? How do you need to change your lifestyle to ensure that you can live longer and healthier? So those are examples of personal goals.

Under my personal goals I might include things like how often I'm planning to work out. I'm a power walker, so I like to set goals around how many miles I want to walk, and how often, during the week. I like to walk at least two to three times a week at the track, or just take a nice, brisk walk through the park. And that is something I enjoy doing.

What I don't do is make a commitment to go the gym every day, or to get on the elliptical machine or to bench press a certain amount of weight, because that's not something I'm interested in or enjoy doing. I know I won't really commit myself to it. I'm not passionate about it.

When I walk, it's great for me. I can walk, talk to myself, reflect, listen to music, think about strategies, think about the day, and it's refreshing to me. So, whatever you like to do in the area of working out, or in personal development, do something you enjoy doing, something you know you can commit to.

Professional Development Goals

Another category of goals might be to focus on your career, on your professional development—that's one of my specific goals. These goals could be things like determining which new skills you need to develop. What skills and strengths do you have that you need to leverage or utilize better? Or one of your goals might be looking for a new job and deciding the specific steps you need to take to get that new job. Another goal might be focused on whether or not you're going to pursue a promotion and how to position yourself to do that. Or, if you are planning to open your own business one day, what are some specific steps you need to take in order to get there, or to get closer to achieving that goal? It might be finding a coach or a mentor, for example. These are a few examples of career and professional goals.

Spiritual Goals

Another category—and for me, the most important category—is spiritual goals. Maybe you use the word "religious," but I think in terms of spiritual goals. This is an important category because the core of who we are and the substance of all the other things I've talked about—mission, purpose, vision—are tied directly to who we are as spiritual beings. These goals have a lot to do with whether or not we want to enhance our internal life, such as our prayer life. Your goal might be to decide if you want to be involved in your church, or how much and to what extent you want to be involved. It may be giving of your time, your talent, and your treasure.

I love to go on mission trips. I like to visit homeless shelters, and I like to help out at food pantries. Bible reading might be a goal that you set. For example, I know that some people commit to reading their Bible in a year, or reading certain Scripture passages over a certain period of time. You may consider attending a women's retreat (or a retreat for men or youth). I love to do those kinds of things. It's something that grounds me and continues to inform the decisions I make. It's a way that helps me stay focused on the right path, pursuing what I believe is the reason I am meant to be here.

With all these categories, you have to look at how you are going to take each goal to the next level. I've been a spiritual person all my life, but I've been especially focused on my spiritual goals over the last 20-plus years. And yet, I'm always looking at how I can make enhancements and improvements to my spiritual life. We should also do that in other areas. How do we make improvements and enhancements to our career and to our professional goals? What do we need to do to reinvent ourselves, to reinvent our personal relationships or our personal development goals? Or what do we need to do better on our jobs and in our professional careers?

All of these goals are important, because if we're not trying to get better, we are stuck, and we'll remain stagnant. So this spiritual goal, especially, is the one that drives and forms and influences all of my other goals.

Financial Goals

Our finances, the fourth area of goal setting, are obviously something that we all care about, because we know that it takes money to make money, but it also takes money just to live on a day-to-day basis. Simple things like having your lights on, being able to talk on the telephone, being able to buy food—these are all things that take money. So money is something that we're always thinking about or hiding from or in denial about, and it's a conversation that we need to have with ourselves.

Some examples of reprioritizing your financial goals might be that you want to establish a budget or that maybe you want to get back on track keeping to your budget. Maybe you didn't have a budget before, or you had one but never really kept it. It could be that your goal is to focus on cutting out certain expenses or perhaps reduce expenses by a certain percent. It could be paying off a certain debt such as—credit cards, student loans, paying down on your mortgage—by making extra payments. Or it might be that you want to attend financial classes or have a financial planner or a financial expert come in and review your finances and help you establish a financial plan to meet your goals.

Financial goals are critical and important and something that I would encourage you to do. And if you have a family, you definitely want to include your spouse, your significant other, or your partner, and even your children in helping you to achieve your financial goals. That is why I've also referred to these as "Team" Goals because it requires a team effort of your household to make it happen.

Family and Household Goals

The last category of goals that I set is my family and household. You may want to sit down with your family to discuss some things that you as a family might work toward together. This is an important conversation to have, and it also will help your children to get into that same habit of planning their lives, making sure that they're laying out specific actions that they're going to take to make things happen. They have to know that life doesn't just come to you and drop things in your lap. We have to teach our children how important it is to plan for success, and that starts with setting goals and making sure that we understand our purpose, our vision and our mission for our own lives.

An example of a goal in the family and household category might be taking or planning a family vacation. That's a goal that goes hand in hand with your financial piece—setting aside money every month, or every paycheck, or however often it is. Whether it's your tax refund or a part of your bonus, you're setting that money aside into a family vacation fund. And a second part of that goal might be that you're allowing your children to participate in where they're going and to plan out specific activities.

Another goal could be getting kids ready for college. I have a daughter in college so this was an important piece for me, not only to ensure that I had her college funds set aside, but also to ensure that her grades stayed on track, that she applied for scholarships, that she got herself in the right mindset, and that she had the discipline she needed make responsible decisions and choices when she went off to college. She is now two years into college, and so far she has proven to be focused, prepared, and disciplined and has earned the designation of Dean's List and National Scholar.

Another family goal might be something like summer camp for the kids. What are some of the things that you're planning as a family for the children to keep them productive and occupied in the summer, and where are some of those specific activities going to be located? It might be that they are going to be visiting their grandparents, or spending time looking for a job, or perhaps they're going to be working part-time over the summer. Or your goal might be attacking those special household projects that you've been wanting to get done for years. Whatever goals you establish, you want to identify: (1) Is it something you can get done within this year? (2) How do you all work together as a family to ensure that it happens?

So these are my five major categories of goals. I identify actions that I'm going to take and I commit to a specific time frame for when I want these things to be accomplished. For example, under personal health and well-being for "when" I will take a walk, I say, "Three times a week I will take a walk." Or I might say, "I am going to ensure that by the June 1st I am going on a family vacation," or "By September 1 I will have this much money saved up toward college," or "I will at least have had a review of my finances." You have to set some specific time frames so that you can hold yourself accountable. **RYW**

"SMART" Goals

I gave you my five major categories. Again, these are personal goals, which I call "me" goals: career and professional goals, health and wellness goals, spiritual goals, financial goals, and family and household goals. I also want to talk about the kinds of goals you need to make, and the things you want to think about when you're setting those goals. You don't just set a goal; you need to be smart about it. You need to set SMART goals.

This is not anything new; you've heard about smart goals before. But I'm going to run through it again, as a reminder. It's important when you're setting smart goals that they be Specific, Measurable, Achievable, Realistic, and Time bound. They have to have a workable time frame.

An example of one of my SMART goals is that "I will take a two-mile power walk twice a week." Now that's very specific. I can measure that because I wear my pedometer and I know when I've hit the two-mile mark. I can look down and see how many calories I've burned, how many steps I've taken, and how many miles I've walked. It's obviously achievable because it's something that I have the resources to do and I have a place where I can go to get it done. It's realistic because it's something that I have the physical capability to achieve. It's realistic because it's something I've done before and it's something I like doing; it's not something I'm going to just get bored with and stop doing all together. Then I talked about setting a realistic time frame. Yes, twice a week is reasonable. It wouldn't be reasonable for me to say that I will commit to walk two miles every single day or twice a day. It's unrealistic because of my hectic travel schedule. The time frame wouldn't allow me to do so. **RYW**

Don't Set Yourself up for Failure

So, I would encourage you to set those kinds of smart goals. Where people often go wrong is when they set goals that are neither specific nor measurable, or not even realistic. For example, one might say, "I am going to lose 20 pounds in 30 days." Well, if you've never worked out; if you haven't adjusted your lifestyle; if you've never lost that much weight in the past; and even if you are overweight now, it's highly unlikely that you're going to lose 20 pounds in 30 days just because you say so. If it's something that you've never done before, you've got take into consideration that you're going to have to make an adjustment mentally as well as physically; you're going to have to make a lifestyle adjustment, and that doesn't come easy. You will not change years of poor diet, lack of exercise, and the wrong mindset in a few days or weeks.

Here's another example of a goal that may not be achievable (and a lot of people set these goals): "I'm going to now go completely vegan." Or "Now I am only going to eat organic foods." Well, if you don't have the finances and this is going to put you way above your budget, you want to rethink that goal. If you don't have a taste for that kind of food, that change in diet, it's going to take time to adjust your taste buds to that kind of food. If you haven't ever learned to cook that kind of food, that's also going to take time.

Again, you have to be realistic and you have to make sure your goal is achievable. Those are smart goals. Don't set goals that are beyond your scope, beyond your reach, your resources, your capability, or your mental capacity. That's how people set themselves up for failure. Set goals around specific things that you're called to do, gifted to do, like to do, are interested in doing, and have the resources to accomplish and the commitment and devotion to be able to make them happen—that is the recipe for success. **RYW**

Summary
- Look back over the past year to identify specific things you have learned, mistakes or missteps you have made, relationships you've been blessed to have. Then find a time and place to reflect on where you need to go next.
- Purpose and vision are all about prioritizing and staying on track, staying focused, and making sure that we're disciplined and directed toward accomplishing our mission in life.
- Setting goals involves setting "Me" goals, such as Health and Wellness, Professional Development, and Spiritual.
- "Team" goals consist of Financial and Family/Household goals.

- SMART goals are Specific, Measurable, Achievable, Realistic, and Time bound—in other words, you can be accountable to yourself in every detail and accomplish your goals in a workable time frame.
- Don't set yourself up for failure by setting goals that are beyond your reach. Set goals around specific things that you're gifted to do, have the resources to accomplish, and the passion for making them happen.

CHAPTER FOUR:
Retooling Your Communication Skills

Effective Communication

EVERY DAY, ALL DAY, WE ARE COMMUNICATING. Whether you agree or disagree, how we communicate is tied directly to our success and to our image. Whether it's verbally or nonverbally, consciously or unconsciously, effectively or ineffectively, we are constantly sending and receiving messages. We're communicating when we speak, when we write a letter, when we walk into a room, when we send an e-mail or a text message, when we make connections on social media such as posting on Twitter, Facebook, Instagram, or LinkedIn, or even when we post a blog. We are constantly sending messages about ourselves. In this chapter, I address strategies for how to achieve success through effective communication, the power of first impressions, different styles of communication, and how to communicate your personal brand.

When I think of great communicators, several examples come to mind. People like Dr. Martin Luther King, Jr., Oprah Winfrey, Joel Osteen, Joyce Myers, Dr. Cornel West, Les Brown, Toni Robbins, Bishop T.D. Jakes, Maya Angelou, and, of course, President Barack Obama and First Lady Michelle Obama—just to name a few. They are powerful, engaging, charismatic, passionate, compelling, purposeful, and dynamic communicators. Effective communication skills are essential for achieving success in your career, your business, personal relationships, social settings, and in every facet of your life.

Toni Robbins, who is a life coach and author, a motivational speaker, and a very effective communicator, states: "To effectively communicate, we must realize that we are all different in the way we perceive the world and the way we use this understanding as a guide to our communication with others." Communication has an impact however it occurs. We use communication to influence every situation, and every interaction in a real and positive way; and how we use it determines its impact. The ability to connect and build rapport with other people is a foundational life skill that should ideally be developed at an early age because it's a learned skill. **RYW**

The Power of First Impressions

When I'm conducting seminars or workshops or giving a keynote speech, or even when I'm talking with clients about this particular topic, I often tell them: "You have less than 30 seconds." Other communication experts have said that you actually have less than 10 seconds. What do you think this means?

This means that when you walk into a room or when you encounter someone, whether it's for a job interview, a new assignment, a promotion, a raise, a special project, a new relationship, or even if you're walking into a bank to get a loan for a new house or a new car, you are being evaluated. And it takes less than 30 seconds for you to be assessed, sized up, and judged. From the clothes you wear to the accessories in your hair, to your shoes, your race, color, shape, and size— people are making assessments about you. They are determining your level of education, your social standing, your level of self-confidence and self-esteem, your financial status, your intellect, your image, your trustworthiness, your credibility—and the list goes on. These determi-

Remember: The *Reinvent Yourself Workbook* provides exercises, reflection questions, and personal assessments based on the material presented in this chapter. WHEN YOU SEE THIS SYMBOL **RYW**, IT MEANS THAT THERE IS A CORRESPONDING EXERCISE OR ACTIVITY FOR YOU TO COMPLETE. Working these exercises will help you to better integrate the material and focus your efforts towards reinventing yourself and achieving success in moving to the next level in your life. Visit **www.drshirleydavis.com/store**.

nations are being made in less than 30 seconds, so chances are that you probably haven't even had an opportunity to speak yet before people have made these evaluations.

First impressions are critical in what we communicate about ourselves to others. A study conducted by the University of Connecticut a few years ago found that first impressions turn out to be 67 percent accurate. You've heard the phrase, "Don't judge a book by its cover." Well, I agree with that notion, but I recognize that we are visual people and we use data to formulate opinions. Good, bad, or indifferent, it is human nature for us to make assessments and determinations about other people. The findings from that research reaffirm the notion that, more often than not, first impressions do matter. In a matter of a few seconds after encountering someone, we can determine whether we're going to invest in a relationship with that person, approve a loan, offer him or her a job, or even give that person our most precious gift, which is our time.

Making a great first impression starts with having a great sense of self-worth and knowing what it is that you have to offer, and then having the ability to be able to project it in a positive and a powerful way. Success starts with self—feeling good about who you are and understanding your purpose and finding meaning in your life.

What Recruiters Look For

I'm in human resources, and I love to study human behavior and how people make decisions. Another survey of recruiters from companies with more than 50,000 employees found that communication skills were cited as the single most important factor in choosing managers and in people's ability to move up in the organization. This study was conducted by the University of Pittsburgh at the Jospeh M. Katz Graduate School of Business. It pointed out that communication skills, including written and oral communication skills, as well as an ability to work with others, are the main factors that contribute to job success.

Over the past 20 years, I've led such functions as recruiting, training and development, diversity, performance management, organizational effectiveness, and employee relations. I agree with the above study, as I've seen many people come in with a very extensive resume of experience; they seem to have the knowledge; they have the skills; and they have the qualifications that we're looking for in the job. But I also find that people who have the ability to make immediate connections, who can articulate their thoughts in a clear, concise and compelling way, who really know how to connect and interact in an effective way through body language, with their gestures and their tone, really do stand out from those who have the resume with the skills, qualifications, and experience, and yet lack the communication piece.

Does What's on Paper Translate into Real Life?

I review countless resumes, and I've had the opportunity to interview hundreds of people seeking a particular job who were a clear match as far as their skills and background were concerned, but talk about first impressions! Some of the applicants would walk into the room looking like they had just woken up; their clothes were wrinkled or they were inappropriately dressed. Others hadn't done their homework and knew very little about the company or the job. They would give incomplete answers and have trouble answering simple behavioral questions like, "Tell me about a time when you had a conflict with another co-worker. How did you deal with it?"

Many looked really impressive on paper. Their resumes were professionally written; they appeared to have the right skills; and their experience and education were documented to match the job description; but when I'd meet with them in person, their body language, communication skills, and personal appearance made a very different impression. It's not enough to look good on paper. Companies want to know that you're professional, polished, that you look the part, and that you will represent their company well. Yes, they want all of that—brains, character, integrity, expertise, and background experience—and they want a professional image. You've got to be able to communicate that in written form, as well as in verbal and nonverbal ways. Yes, companies want the whole package, and that's fair, because as individuals we're looking for the whole package as well. We want to work for a great company that has competitive pay and great benefits, a company that provides growth and development opportunities, has a good reputation, and a great work culture and environment.

Your Communication Can Be a Deal Breaker

But how are you communicating in the interview? Could the way you communicate be the deal breaker for why you didn't get the job? Ask yourself: Is it because of what I wore that I didn't get the job? Could it have been the way I walked into the interview and shook hands, or didn't shake hands? Or maybe I didn't make eye contact or my sentences were run-on, or maybe I used poor grammar. Maybe I was using slang and street jargon, and maybe I really didn't answer the questions completely. My clothes could've been too tight. Maybe my pants were too baggy. Or maybe I showed too much cleavage or my shoes looked run over. Or maybe it was my smell. All of these things enter into a person's decision in the first 10, 20, 30 seconds that you walk into a room. And it's all important.

I will let you in on a little secret. As someone who reviews resumes and brings people in for interviews, I can tell you that when people walk into an interview, we are making these assessments in the first couple of seconds. We are literally deciding right then and there, and certainly within those first 20 to 30 seconds, whether or not you are a right fit. Remember, as recruiters and interviewers, we are making decisions about whether or not we will give you our company's time or money—or, specifically, a job. During those first 30 seconds, we're looking at whether or not a person is going to be a serious candidate or if we're basically just going to give them a courtesy interview; and a lot of that is determined by how you walk into the room—how you carry yourself and what your appearance portrays.

If your interview lasts only five or ten minutes, and no more than fifteen, chances are you didn't make a good first impression, and the company didn't see you projecting the image they were looking for.

We'll discuss in more detail about making an impression and packaging ourselves in a way that people really do see that we are the material and the package they're looking for. You may have all the credentials, and you may have more than enough knowledge to do the job, but if the interviewer can't get past those first things—that you're not dressed appropriately, or your speech or your grammar is poor, or you're just not making a connection, or you're not able to articulate in an effective way—those things play into the decision whether you're hired or just given a courtesy interview.

Body Language Studies—The 7%–38%–55% Rule

Albert Mehrabian, currently professor emeritus of psychology at UCLA, has become known best by his publications on the relative importance of verbal and nonverbal messages (aka the "body language studies). His findings on inconsistent messages of feelings and attitudes have been quoted throughout human communication seminars worldwide, and have also become known as the 7%-38%-55% rule He found that only seven percent of the emotional meaning in a message is composed of the actual words that we use. So consider the following statistics about how we communicate. Seven percent of the way we communicate is through words—words only. Thirty-eight percent of our communication is through the tone of voice we use and our voice inflection. That means that 55 percent of the way we communicate comes through nonverbal communication—our body language. We're talking about facial expressions, gestures, and posture. This startling statistic reminds us that others believe the visual information we make available to them before they believe the content of the words we use.

What You See Is What You Believe

It's not so much what we say. It's not so much even how we say it. More importantly, it's what we look like when we're projecting the message—that's what people believe. They believe what the communicator is showing them, more so than what the communicator is telling them.

Nonverbal language is one of the most vital parts of communication, especially if we see that it's 55 percent of the way we communicate. How often have you been able to determine what somebody is really saying just by reading their facial expression?

The context of the situation often gives away the clue. Try this exercise. Turn down the volume when you're watching a movie. The body language and the facial expressions provide information about whether the movie is a comedy, a love story, or a horror flick. You can often tell just by looking at the characters rather than listening to the words. Or watch a sporting event. You can easily determine who in the stands is rooting for which team by the jerseys, the caps, and the paraphernalia the majority of fans are wearing. You can also determine who's a sports enthusiast and who's a casual observer. You can see by the way they respond to the game. You can see their body language and reactions when a referee calls a play against their team. You can see their energy level, their posture, and their facial expression; and all those things will give you clues as to which team is winning or which team might be losing.

Do you ever go people watching? I love to watch people at the park or at the mall, or sometimes when I'm in a restaurant where I can just sit down and look at people. Here's another exercise. Observe people in a restaurant. You might see a group of men and women dressed in suits dining together in the middle of the day. That often signifies that it's a team meeting or some kind of working lunch. Or you might see a man and a woman having a candlelight dinner and holding hands. While they're talking to each other and looking into each other's eyes, what assumptions might you make? You might assume that it's date night, or that it might be their first date, or that they're just madly in love and this is an early stage of the relationship. You might assume all kinds of things. You might also see in another part of the restaurant that there's a mom with five children in an area that's decorated with balloons and cake, and you may assume that there's a birthday celebration or some kind of other special event.

We are always making assessments by just looking at people— looking at their expressions, at their body language, at the way that they dress, and at the way that they look. We don't always talk to them. We don't know what they're saying in their private conversations, but we do make assumptions. Now assume that this same thing is happening with you whenever people look at you. We all use nonverbal communication unconsciously, all the time.

Fifty-five percent of our communication is nonverbal, as we quoted from the above survey. To project a more impactful presence through our nonverbal communication, we have to start by examining our own level of competency in certain levels.

First: How do you enter a room? Are you noticed when you walk into a room? Do you offer your hand immediately, regardless of the person's gender, race, size, or color? Do you make eye contact when you greet people and throughout the conversation? Do you have any distracting gestures that get in the way of people being able to fully connect with you? Are you aware of how you show nervousness under stress? Are the nonverbal messages you send really clear, or are people always confused about where they stand with you? Could it be that they don't know what kind of person you are or what to expect from you because of the mixed messages you're sending?

Our physical presence, our posture, handshake, eye contact—these are the first body language characteristics that other people get a chance to see; and they're usually evaluating our performance in each of these areas. So what is it that you could do differently to better enhance your nonverbal communication skills and your presence? Let's address this in terms of presence and passion and energy.

When you think of people you know who command presence every time they walk into a room, what is it about them that's different? What do you think about when those people walk into the room? They command presence; they have a certain aura. But what is it about them? What exactly do they do that makes other people take notice? Think about a time when you watched an entertainer's performance. What was it that impressed you about that performance? What did they do to command that attention? Was it perhaps the way they came onto the stage? Was it the way they immediately connected? Was it what they were wearing? Think about the last speaker you heard in the same way—how did they come onto the stage? How did they connect with you? How did they command the audience and get your attention? Was it something that they were wearing? What did they do? **RYW**

Communication is About the "It" Factor

This is a phenomenon that researchers and business professionals continue to study. We're always looking at what makes people have what they have, whether it's called the "it" factor or the "wow" factor. Corporate America sometimes calls it "executive presence" or "leadership presence"; or they just call it an "aura." It's something you don't always know how to completely describe, but you know it when you see it. We all are made up of some form of energy and we're always giving off that level of energy to others wherever we go. Whether we're speaking to them or just walking past them or just observing them, there is an energy that we are putting out.

Whether we're talking about professional or executive presence, or we're talking about the "it" factor or the "wow" factor, it is all about exuding that kind of powerful, professional, and effective energy that connects people and draws them into our sphere of influence. We all have different styles in the way we communicate, and we all have different levels of energy. The best communicator is not necessarily someone who is extroverted with a hyped personality and a lot of passion, like me. I'm a "type A" personality and I communicate outwardly with my hands and with gestures. I come across with a lot of passion and I like to project in a very strong, confident way. But an effective communicator can also be someone who's quieter and more reserved, and who projects a calm energy. I'm reminded of Maya Angelou. She's someone like that, a very effective communicator, yet quiet and unassuming; she's a sweet soul and quite introverted, but when she hits the stage and opens her mouth she is very impactful in the way she communicates and in the way she captivates audiences.

The other area of nonverbal communication—and remember, that's 55 percent of the way we communicate—is the nonverbal gestures we make. We addressed posture and walking into a room, but making eye contact is equally important. It's the way people connect with you. We often say that the eyes are the windows to the soul. Well, eye contact is a powerful way to establish trust and rapport, and even credibility and comfort. The effective use of eye contact helps people to exhibit confidence as a speaker and respect for the listener. **RYW**

Dominant Communication Styles

Next, I want to address the various styles of communication. I noted that we have various types and levels of passion. Just as we have different styles of communication, we also have different personality styles— we even have different thinking styles, but I want to focus on the styles of communication, and I want you to see if you find yourself in one or more of these, given the context or given a certain situation. Most of us have a dominant communication style. So take this opportunity to self-assess and to reflect on where you fall on the communications scale and whether or not your communication style is effective.

You may find this a little uncomfortable as I describe each style, because some of them can be destructive, and certainly not the best styles to have, but you may identify with a particular style. This is a good time to set some goals and to create a development plan for how you can shift from being an ineffective communicator to being a very effective one. Use this as a coaching session—as an opportunity to grow and to develop yourself.

The Aggressive Communicator

The first style is the aggressive communicator. Aggressive communicators express their feelings and their opinions, and they advocate for their own needs and their own wants in a way that violates the rights of others. They are verbally and sometimes physically abusive, which is born out of low self-esteem. Oftentimes, it's caused by having experienced some past physical or emotional abuse; it can even come from unhealed emotional wounds or unresolved issues, or from having feelings of powerlessness. An aggressive communication style involves some form of manipulation, because you want to get your way. It's as if you're fighting out something that's happened to you by fighting others or taking it out on them. Whether it's from something in your past, in your recent history, or even if it's going on now, by using this kind of communication style you are attempting to make people do what you want done by inducing some kind of guilt, hurt, intimidation, and/or control tactics.

Have you ever been around a person like that? I can recall having bosses like that; they were very aggressive and they ruled with an iron fist. They always seemed to live by this mantra: "It's my way or the highway and no other way at all." Have you ever been in personal relationships where the person has tried to impose that same kind of power over you? It's often because they themselves feel powerless. It's like high school bullying. Bullies try to control other people because they're deflecting from some personal powerlessness that they feel themselves.

Whether covertly or overtly, the aggressive communicator wants to have their needs met—and right now. The aggressive communicator often tries to dominate other people. They use humiliation to control; they criticize, blame, and attack others; but they won't take personal responsibility themselves. They can be impulsive. They have a low frustration and tolerance level. They speak in a loud, demanding, and sometimes overbearing voice. They don't listen well. They interrupt frequently. They use statements like: "You always do this." "You did this to me." "You this and you that." They are constantly making piercing eye contact and demonstrating an overbearing posture that's offensive and hard to control.

The Impact of Being an Aggressive Communicator

Let's address the impact of this communication style. Sometimes, individuals become alienated from others, or they alienate themselves from people. They try to enclose others or keep them from being around other people. They generate fear and hatred in others. They blame other people instead of taking responsibility for their own issues, and they paralyze themselves from being able to grow and mature. Not only will the aggressive communicator use "you" words, but they flip the script and use other words to make you feel inferior, that you're the one who's wrong. They may use phrases like: "I'm superior." "I'm right." "I can violate your rights." "I can dominate you and I can intimidate you." "I'll get my way no matter what," or "You're not worth anything." "It's all your fault." I'm entitled." "You owe me because I own you." These are the kinds of destructive and aggressive statements or behaviors that you'll hear from this style of communicator.

If you find yourself using this kind of communication style most of the time, that's most likely your dominant style. I can tell you that it's not effective at all. And, as I suggested above, use this as a coaching session—as a private time for personal reflection and self-assessment, to look at yourself in the mirror and make a change. These behaviors are certainly not effective in the workplace. Neither are they effective at home, in your personal relationships, or in any other arena of your life. They will probably make you feel bad about yourself, and they don't work all the time. What you often find yourself doing then is taking it out on others or lashing out with verbal attacks only to try and make yourself feel better, but it doesn't heal the problem.

The Passive Communicator

The second communication style is called the passive communicator. This is a person who has developed a pattern of avoidance. These individuals avoid expressing their own opinions or feelings; they protect their own rights, identify and meet their own needs. Passive communicators won't necessarily seek to have their own way, but they are often born with low self-esteem as well, just like the aggressive communicator—except these individuals actually believe they're not worthy. Their communication style is based on compliance and hoping to avoid confrontation at all costs. In this mode of communication they don't necessarily talk much; they question even less; and they actually do very little. They usually don't want to rock the boat, and they have learned that it's easier and safer not to react, that it's better to disappear than to stand up and confront the issue. As a result, passive communicators don't respond openly or clearly or even visibly. They usually don't want to respond or to deal with hurtful and anger-inducing situations. Instead, they allow grievances and annoyances to mount up and fester, unaware even that they're building up.

We know too what can happen when a person who's allowed things to go on and on and fester. It often builds up inside and the person becomes a walking, ticking time bomb; you just never know at what point this person will explode. And when they do explode, you feel like: "Gosh. Where did that come from?" It's confusing because they haven't shared with you anything that was going on or anything they were feeling; they haven't confronted the issues, but they have allowed them to build up over time. Once they reach this breaking point or this high tolerance threshold for unacceptable behavior, they have an explosive outburst, which is usually out of proportion or out of control, or even out of sorts. You just happened to be the last straw that broke the camel's back in the situation, or you happened to be there at the wrong time to witness this outburst. Afterward, they feel ashamed; they feel guilty and confused; yet they then go back to being very passive.

The Impact of Being a Passive Communicator

Passive communicators often fail to stand up for themselves, and they allow others to deliberately infringe on their rights. They fail to express their feelings and tend to speak softly or apologetically; they also exhibit poor eye contact and poor body posture. You can imagine the impact this communication style can have. Often, the individual is feeling anxious because life seems out of control. They sometimes feel depressed because they feel stuck and hopeless. They feel resentful and sometimes are not even aware of that resentment because their needs are not being met.

And they feel confused, because they ignore their own feelings and are unable to grow and to develop and mature because they never address the real issues. They have more unresolved issues than they ever resolve.

The impact of that is that passive communicators will believe or say to themselves that they are unable to stand up for their rights. They may say things like: "I don't know what my rights are." "I get stepped on by everybody all the time." "I am such a pushover." "I'm weak." "I'm unable to take care of myself." "I can't do this." "I can't do that." So when you're around people who are constantly saying what they can't do, they come across as self-deprecating. These are the people we call passive communicators; they never seem to consider their own feelings, but then there comes a breaking point at which they explode. It is definitely not an effective communication style.

The Passive-Aggressive Communicator

The third style is the passive-aggressive communicator. These individuals appear passive on the surface, but they act out their anger in a subtle, indirect, behind-the-scenes, behind-your-back way. On the surface, they appear passive; they don't necessarily want to have to deal with things, or they avoid things, but in a behind-your-back way they act out when they don't think you're looking. For example, they might believe that they have the right to their own beliefs and opinions, but they don't express them openly. Instead, they might resort to masking their communication or taking actions behind your back and causing conflicts indirectly; or they may be nonresponsive all together and get even in an indirect way. The passive-aggressive communication style usually produces stress and doesn't help resolve issues—it actually helps expand the issues and conflicts.

People who develop this pattern of passive-aggressiveness exhibit a combination of the passive and aggressive styles, They feel powerless; they feel stuck; they feel resentment; they haven't dealt with issues; they feel incapable of dealing with the object of their resentment, so instead they express it through anger and other ways that aren't healthy.

Passive-aggressive communicators will often monitor themselves rather than confront the person or the issue. They have difficultly acknowledging their anger or they are in denial about it. They use facial expressions that don't match how they feel. They might be smiling when they are really ticked off, or they use sarcasm. They may even deny that there's a problem and appear cooperative, when in fact they're doing things to annoy, disrupt, sabotage, or even get even.

The Impact of Being a Passive-Aggressive Communicator

The impact of the passive-aggressive communication style is not positive at all. These individuals become alienated from other people and they lose friends. They feel stuck. They feel powerless. They discharge resentment while never addressing or dealing with real issues. They have a lot of unresolved issues and sometimes carry a lot of baggage, and a lot of grudges, and they let things fester. People exhibiting this style may appear cooperative, but they really won't cooperate. They may say yes to your face but behind your back they won't follow through or they won't commit or deliver on what they said. Again, this is not a healthy, effective communication style. You can easily understand how the behaviors can be career limiting or even career ending—they will certainly impact your ability to be successful.

The passive-aggressive style is not effective at work, nor is it effective at home. How many times have you said something to your children, and they act as if they're listening, and they say: "Got it," or "Yeah, I understand," or "Yeah, Mom, I'll do it," and when you come back to see if they've done what they said they were going to do, it just didn't happen. They acted like they were going to do it, or they pretended that they totally understood, but then they play dumb when you come back and ask them, "Why didn't you do it?" or "Didn't you understand what I said?"

Even in personal relationships when you are talking, the other person may act like they're listening or they give off vibes and project body language like they are, but they're really tuning you out on the inside. They may be very engaged in the conversation with you but when they leave they're talking to themselves or they're whispering something that is obviously what they meant to say, but they didn't say to you. So these are not effective, healthy ways to build relationships on the job, and certainly not at home.

The Assertive Communicator

I saved the healthiest and most effective form of communication for last. It's the assertive communicator. This is how we naturally express ourselves when our self-esteem is intact, when we feel good about ourselves, when we have good self-confidence, and when we are able to communicate to others without playing games, without manipulation, without control, and without the need to sabotage. The assertive communicator has the ability to state their feelings, opinions, and needs. People who are assertive communicators are able to be firm, and they're able to express their rights without violating the rights of others. They have a great sense of self-worth, and they are emotionally and spiritually strong. They are aware of their physical, emotional, and mental needs and capacities. They are respectful of others because they have a great sense of self-respect.

There are a couple of things you might hear from assertive communicators. They state their needs and they state their wants very clearly, but always appropriately and in a respectful way. They know how to use tact and how to be politically correct. They use "I" statements instead of "you" statements to avoid placing blame. When you're talking to somebody, you really start to place the blame when you say, "You always," "You never," or "You didn't," versus saying, "I need to better understand," or "I can accept that," or "Here's where I may have gone wrong," or "Here's what I was thinking." These are phrases that disarm a conversation that has the potential of going awry or creating conflict.

The Impact of Being an Assertive Communicator

Assertive communicators listen well without interrupting; they make good eye contact; they speak in a very clear tone of voice; and they have a relaxed body posture. They feel connected to other people and they feel competent to stand up for their rights, and they don't have a problem standing up for the rights of others as well. The assertive communication style is obviously the best way to communicate. It's an effective style that you should be espousing, striving for, and developing over time.

These are the four communication styles: aggressive, passive, passive-aggressive, and assertive. Where do you find yourself among the four styles? Are you a passive-aggressive communicator? Or do you consider yourself, for the most part, an assertive communicator? What is your most significant communication behavior? Do you tend to be the dominant communicator? When you fall into your natural habit, which of these communication styles do you fall into?

Obviously, at some point in some situations, we can find ourselves using one of the unhealthy and ineffective communication styles. There have been times when I've experienced myself being very passive, when I just didn't want to deal with something. I was over it; I was tired; it had just been a long day; it wasn't a battle I wanted to fight or a hill I wanted to die on; so I was passive. I didn't say anything and just walked away. There have been times when I've been very aggressive, when I knew that something offended me, or bothered me, and I needed to deal with it; I needed to be very strong, and I needed to control the situation.

There have even been times when I've been in a passive-aggressive situation as well. It may have been that I expressed my opinion or that I didn't agree with something and the other person had authority over me. I didn't agree. And, yes, there have been times when I've walked back and I've said what I needed to say to someone else; or I closed the door and said it to myself in the bathroom or in my office, and I didn't follow through on it and hoped that it would just go away. That happens in a lot of corporations. When people are not in agreement with a certain change or they don't like a certain leader or manager's style, they tend to be very passive-aggressive.

So let's acknowledge that we sometimes fall into other modes of communication. Let's be real with ourselves. At the same time, however,

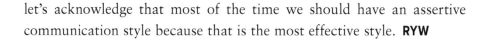

let's acknowledge that most of the time we should have an assertive communication style because that is the most effective style. **RYW**

Listening—A Key Ingredient to Effective Communication

Before I leave this segment I want to address another aspect of effective communication, and that is active listening. I can't say enough about how important active listening is. It is a key ingredient to being successful. You have to hear what people are really saying, and you have to be able to respond so that people know that you are listening and that you care. People don't always care about what you know, but they really do want to know that you care. That's an important ingredient in relationships, and certainly it's an important piece in business relationships.

Listening is one of the most important, yet under-utilized skills that we need to build as leaders and that we demonstrate as individuals. How well do you listen? If you think about it, do you listen more than you talk? Or as I heard someone say: "We need to listen proportionately to the way that we were designed." This means that we have two ears and one mouth, and we should listen proportionately; we obviously need to spend more time being better listeners and being active listeners.

How Much Do You Hear?

Most people think they are good listeners, but in fact they're not. We remember about 25 to 50 percent of what we hear—no more than 50 percent. This means that when you talk to your boss or colleagues or customers or a spouse or a child or your partner or your significant other for about ten minutes, you can really only remember about two and a half to five minutes of the conversation. It's funny. And it's been a learning experience for me as well. For example, when you get out of church you feel like, "Yeah, that was a really good message. The pastor did a great job." Then somebody asks, "Oh, what did he talk about?" And you can't remember; you just heard it 10 to 15 minutes before, and you can't really recall what was said.

It was a good message, for sure, but, again, we don't tend to retain much of the information once we've left the venue. This is why it's important to address active listening. We go in to a meeting sometimes, maybe at the office, and have a conversation with someone. We can never recall everything that person said, certainly not verbatim. You may recall the context, or you may even be able to paraphrase what they said but, remember, we also have our own filters. We're often listening from our own context and, when we repeat what we think we understood the other person is saying, we sometimes miss the message because we were listening from our own understanding and not listening to understand. So that resonates statistically; we really only remember about 25 to 50 percent of what we hear.

There are a number of reasons why we should listen. We should listen to obtain information, to hear, to understand, and even just for greater enjoyment. We could be listening to a symphony or listening to a song or listening to someone recite a poem. Whatever it might be, there are reasons for why we listen. Clearly, listening is a skill that everyone can benefit from and a skill we all need to improve. By becoming a better listener, you improve your productivity and your ability to influence and connect with other people. Listening builds greater, stronger, healthier relationships, because people want to know that you care. The way you demonstrate your care and concern is by listening and being able to repeat back or reflect back what you heard others say. Listening skills can also help you to avoid conflicts and minimize misunderstandings. All of these are important in our careers, our relationships—in every aspect of our lives.

Your takeaways here are that (1) our communication style is important, and being an assertive communicator is the most important style; (2) it is important that we are aware and practice great body language—55 percent of our communication is driven by our body language; and (3) most of all, it's important that we practice the key communication skill, being an active listener. **RYW**

Your Attitude Communicates Louder Than Words

The last ingredient to effective communication that I want to address is attitude. Attitude is either good or bad—there is no in-between. I don't know about you but I have met a number of people in my life who needed an attitude adjustment. Do you need one? Has anyone ever told you that you need to have an attitude adjustment? Let's put it this way: Your attitude can determine your altitude. The better your attitude, the higher you will go in life, because a bad attitude, as we know, can take the wind out of your sails. It's like sticking a pin in a balloon. It's like a cancer. If you've ever been around a negative person or a person with a bad attitude, or even a person who has been infected or influenced by someone else with a bad attitude, it starts to rub off.

I've been involved with coworkers who are negative. I have family members who have bad attitudes. I even remember dating a guy who had such a negative attitude that it got to the point I didn't even want to be around him anymore. It didn't matter how cute he was or how spiritual he appeared or how educated he was or that he had a great job or what we had in common. His bad attitude was a complete turnoff. Everything was wrong with the world; he always complained about things; there was nothing he could find good in. It produced such negative energy for me that I ended that relationship.

Need an Attitude Adjustment?

The point here is that if you have a bad attitude, you've got to make an attitude adjustment because it will cost you time, money, relationships, career, and success. If you have people in your life who are close to you and part of your inner circle, you have to make sure that you are not allowing their bad attitude to rub off on you. In fact, I would submit to you that you might want to reconsider having any negative people in your inner circle, because those closest to us tend to rub off on us. They influence us, whether it's negative, good, bad, or indifferent. So, if you have people around you who have a bad attitude, you might want to think about gathering another set of good friends in your inner circle.

It is important to have the right people in your life and to make sure that you pick the right relationships. (I will address this further in Chapter 6.) Make sure that you eliminate from your inner circle those people who will take you down, those people who speak negative things, who don't believe in you, who don't help build you up, but who are always finding reasons why you can't do anything. Those people are toxic, unhealthy, and ineffective. You have to make sure that you're selecting the right people who will be able to speak the right things in your life to help build your life and who are also able to hold you accountable for when you have a bad attitude, or when you're not actively listening, or when you're not being an effective communicator. In other words, it's important that we think about the circle of friends we have around us and make sure that we have people who have great attitudes, people who are looking out for our best interests, people who have our back, and people who will call us on the carpet when we're not doing what we should be doing.

Before I end this chapter, it's appropriate that I touch on personal branding, which we'll cover in the next chapter on rebuilding your career. I've covered communication skills and how you present yourself and how you make first impressions. Whether it's for your career or for personal relationships, personal branding is a critical skill. There are a number of ways you can promote your personal brand, and they fall basically into two categories: One way is how you present yourself personally, face to face. The other way is how you present yourself online and in written communications. I will address career branding and how important it is to market yourself. We all project a particular brand or a particular image in the way we present ourselves to other people. **RYW**

Let's Review

In the first chapter, you defined what success means for you; in the second chapter, you examined how to understand your purpose and your vision and began to walk in that understanding; in the third chapter, you identified how important it is to set achievable goals that are tied directly back to your purpose and your vision. All of that affects the image you present, your personal brand, and what you want other people to know about you. How are you carrying yourself? What aura are you giving off? It's a critical skill that most people underutilize or don't use at all. It's a skill that is usually undervalued because people don't necessarily know how to do it, and because it has a lot to do with how people see you and, more importantly, with how you see yourself first.

Summary

- Communication has an impact in all our interactions and influences every situation— how we use it determines its impact. Effective communication builds rapport with other people and is a foundational life skill that should be developed at an early age.

- When you walk into a room or when you encounter someone, it takes less than 30 seconds for you to be assessed, sized up, and judged. First impressions are critical in what we communicate about ourselves to others.

- The 7%-38%-55% rule states that seven percent of the way we communicate is through words, thirty-eight percent is through the tone of voice we use and our voice inflection, and 55 percent comes through nonverbal communication—our body language.

- The "it" factor or the "wow" factor is all about exuding a powerful, professional, and effective energy that connects people and draws them into our sphere of influence.

- Most of us have a dominant communication style, so take this opportunity to self-assess and to reflect on whether or not your communication style is effective. Here are the five styles:

  » Aggressive communicators express their feelings and their opinions in a way that violates the rights of others.

  » Passive communicators develop a pattern of avoidance; they avoid expressing their own opinions or feelings; they protect their own rights and meet their own needs.

» Passive-aggressive communicators appear passive on the surface, but they act out their anger in subtle, indirect, behind-the-scenes ways.

» Assertive communicators exhibit the healthiest and most effective form of communication; they naturally feel good about themselves; their self-esteem is intact; and they don't play games or try to manipulate when they communicate.

- Listening is the key ingredient to effective communication—and to success.

- Attitude—good or bad—speaks louder than words.

CHAPTER FIVE:
Rebuilding Your Career

Seasons of Change

ARE YOU AT A POINT IN YOUR LIFE now where you have become much more aware of time? Do you appreciate time more? Do you recognize how fast time seems to pass us by—and how quickly times are changing?

I was in a telephone conversation the other day with my mom, just catching up on the family and seeing how this one was doing and how that one was doing. You know how mothers and daughters are. We talk about who's getting married and who's getting divorced, or who's having a baby and who's graduating from high school or college, or who's got a new job or who just loss their job—all the family catch up. As we were talking about my daughter, I had this nostalgic feeling come over me, "Wow, it seemed like just yesterday I was telling my mom that I was pregnant." It seemed like just yesterday I was holding this newborn baby in my arms. It seemed like just yesterday I was watching her take her first steps. Yet, we found ourselves on the phone talking about how she's doing in college. Just a few years ago I saw my daughter graduate from high school and then I saw her off to college, and now we're talking about what she'll do after graduation from college.

I thought, "Wow! How quickly times have changed." Just two years ago I wasn't married and now I am; I was a single mom, and now I have two stepchildren. My body is going through changes now that I'm married and getting older, because I have changed my lifestyle. I'm cooking more, I'm eating more, and I'm putting on a few extra pounds. I'm much more conscientious about my weight now than I was before I got married, but I'm finding it harder and harder to keep it off.

At some point, we all become a little more conscientious about our health and our wellness. We spend more money on vitamins, healthy foods, hair care products, and doctor appointments, trying to maintain some semblance of youthfulness. As we get older, most of us start to wish that time would slow down and that things wouldn't change so quickly. But the winds of change are rapidly blowing and we're experiencing a dramatic shift not only in our own personal lives, but also in our careers. As a global human resources and workforce management expert, I study workforce trends. It's important to know how the workforce has been shifting over time because it impacts how we need to shift in rebuilding our careers and our organizations.

The Workforce Is Changing

Think about the changes that have occurred over the last few years. You see more and more women entering into the workforce. In fact, nearly 51 percent of the U.S. population is women already (globally it's nearly 50%). There are more people of color coming into the workforce—African-Americans, Latinos, Hispanics, Asian-Americans, American-Indians, immigrants from other countries. Four generations are working alongside each other, which means that there are new rules, new approaches, new strategies, and new ways of working and thinking—new paradigms and new models of practice that we have to adopt.

Technology is changing at the speed of light. In his book, *The World Is Flat: A Brief History of the Twenty-First Century,* (Farrar,

Remember: The *Reinvent Yourself Workbook* provides exercises, reflection questions, and personal assessments based on the material presented in this chapter. WHEN YOU SEE THIS SYMBOL **RYW**, IT MEANS THAT THERE IS A CORRESPONDING EXERCISE OR ACTIVITY FOR YOU TO COMPLETE. Working these exercises will help you to better integrate the material and focus your efforts towards reinventing yourself and achieving success in moving to the next level in your life. Visit **www.drshirleydavis.com/store**.

Straus and Giroux, 2005), Thomas Friedman writes about how fast technology has shifted and changed. Ten years ago Facebook didn't even exist; LinkedIn was a term that was used to describe prison; a cloud was something we saw in the sky; an app was something we would send in for a job or to apply to college; and Skype was considered a typo. Can you imagine that just ten years ago we weren't even thinking about an iPhone or an iPad or an iPod. Now it's a worldwide phenomenon, and you see long lines of very committed customers every time a new one is released. It has almost become a culture. And look at how quickly technology is redefining the way we communicate, the way we meet people or do business, and even the way we find jobs.

The job market is tighter than ever. For four years or more, we have experienced unemployment over eight percent. While it is declining now (at least as of this writing) there's still so much uncertainty in our economic situation that has a direct impact on the job market, which ultimately has an impact on our own careers. Companies have been going through a lot of shifts and changes as the economy has changed; they have undergone workforce reductions, pay cuts, budget cuts, hiring freezes, and all kinds of strategic business maneuvers to reposition themselves and see how they might pivot so they can better function in the new world economy. All these changes have left us questioning our own careers and our own jobs. **RYW**

Steps to Rebuilding Your Career

You may be asking yourself, "Is this the right job for me?" Do I want to continue to work in this toxic culture or this toxic work environment? Do I want to continue to report and work under this bad boss? Am I making enough money, or can I go somewhere and make more? Is now the time to start my own business? Is now the time to put my talents or skills to use doing something I've always wanted to do but never had the time or never thought I could do?" Or are you waiting for the tides to turn, for the economy to recover so there will be more job opportunities for you to consider? Maybe you're even considering going back to school to learn a new skill or to learn a new trade. We all get to some stage or season in our lives when we have to ponder these same questions. We have to adopt new strategies, develop a new mindset, set new goals, and even do a complete makeover—in our career, our relationships, our finances, and even our spiritual life.

Now is the time to consider how we rebuild our career in the midst of these workforce shifts and changing circumstances. Whether we were aware and forewarned and had time to prepare and plan, or we were completely blindsided and caught off guard, now is the time to embrace the change. We all know that change is inevitable and we've got to learn how to embrace the change and not be paralyzed by it.

Embrace Change

This is the first step we have to take toward rebuilding our career or reinventing ourselves. Be willing to embrace change and look at it as an opportunity and not as our enemy or as an imposition, and certainly not as a defeat. How would you react if you walked into your workplace and you were told that you were being laid off and that today was your last day? Millions of Americans have faced this same fate over the last four years. After you get past the initial shock, anger, resentment, bitterness, and blaming, it's time to turn those negative emotions into something positive, which brings me to step number two.

Avoid Pity Parties

Avoid being around people who are negative. In these circumstances, they are toxic. Make sure that you surround yourself with your closest friends, those who really support you; those who can speak to life and speak positive things; those who can help you feel better about the situation. It's easy for us to feel bad about ourselves and to get down on ourselves for what we didn't do; we start to experience low self-esteem; and we fall into a "woe is me" attitude. It's important at this time to build yourself up in your faith and to surround yourself with great friends who are able to give you positive energy and help you to look at this in a different, very positive light.

Don't Get Bitter, Get Better!

This is the third step: Capitalize on the time you have, whether by taking a class and learning a new skill or by deciding to go back to school to get a degree, or by developing a skill in a vocational trade that you didn't have before. You may even utilize some of those other talents and hobbies that you have been wanting to use but never did because your job didn't afford you the time. It may even allow you time to produce some additional revenue. This may now be the opportunity for you to go into business for yourself and to do that very thing you've always dreamed about doing. It could be your opportunity to be a consultant and to work with different companies and different projects and learn different industries. There are any number of ways that you can utilize the time you have, but most importantly: Don't get bitter; you have to get better!

Turn Your Contacts into Contracts

Another step toward rebuilding your career, especially during a time of setback, is to get out your contact list. If that list is limited, this is the time to develop the right relationships, build the right networks, and turn your contacts into contracts. When you are experiencing a setback or a transition in your career, it's a great opportunity to draw on the relationships you've been building from networking events that you've attended, from business cards you've collected, from connections you've made on social media, or however you made new relationships and new contacts. Look for recruiters or headhunters, people you know who may be able to access new job opportunities or refer you to people in the right companies. Even look for people who have certain skill sets you don't have, and use this as an opportunity to receive more mentoring and to learn new skills.

Inventory Your Strengths

The next thing you want to do is to inventory your strengths, your skill sets, your abilities, and your experience. This is an important piece. This is what you get when you go through an out-placement service. But let's assume you don't receive that service. This was your last day at work, and you just found out that they're not providing you any additional services. You've got to be able to think for yourself: "What do I do next?" One of the things you want to do is to think about how you develop now, how you capitalize on your existing strengths and skills. This could mean examining your background. It could mean dusting off and updating your resume. It could mean talking to people who mentored you in the past or coworkers who worked closely with you. It could mean revisiting some of your previous performance reviews and other assessments to identify what your strengths are, what results you achieved, and what areas were consistently identified as development areas or shortcomings. And it is an opportunity to look at ways you can start to build your personal brand, market yourself, and make yourself viable and visible in the job market.

Here's a job-searching tip: Make sure that you define the types of jobs that match your skills. If you are not very savvy on the computer, you're at a disadvantage. I would encourage you to post your resume on a number of different online job boards. Most companies are now recruiting people from online. They are not necessarily interested in you cold-calling them, sending in your application by hand, or walking it in to the personnel department. This is the age of the Internet. You have to be on a number of different job sites, whether it's Monster.com, Ladders, LinkedIn, or CareerBuilder, or specialized industries that have job boards. They make job announcements on many different social media outlets.

I spend a lot of time in the social media space, and I'm constantly seeing people announcing jobs on Twitter. I see them on Facebook. I see them listed in LinkedIn—and if you go to the LinkedIn website, look under specific jobs. You can join a number of different groups that are on social media specifically for networking about new job opportunities. You might join a community club or a specific industry organization where you can go to luncheons or attend specific seminars. Again, these are opportunities to network. And that's a critical skill to possess when you're rebuilding your career.

Perhaps you don't want to do the same thing you've been doing. For example, if you've been a recruiter, maybe now you're interested in going into the IT field. Or, if you're a banker, maybe you're considering going into education. Ask yourself, do you have transferable skills from the one job over to the next job? Often, people apply for the same kind of job they were in, not realizing that they may be able to apply for jobs in a number of different kinds of career paths—jobs that may not necessarily be in the field they were in but that require the skill sets they have. You have to be able to communicate and translate those skills that are needed and useful. You may have been in healthcare, for example, working as a receptionist in one of the hospitals. You can be a receptionist in any other industry; those are transferrable skills. Or maybe you are a computer technician and are able to perform data analysis and build websites. You may even be able to do some consulting. That firm may be closing that particular job opportunity, but that doesn't mean you couldn't do some personal consulting. There are many people looking to have websites built and companies that are outsourcing their IT department because they have more needs than skills available.

Reestablish Your Personal Brand

I addressed personal branding and marketing above and how important they are in this job market. Because of the current unemployment rates, one of the trends I'm seeing is that for every job posted there are hundreds and hundreds of resumes submitted. The other trend I'm seeing is that, because people have been unemployed for so long, those who used to be in mid- and senior-level positions are now willing to take jobs at a much lower level and with much lower pay than what they were accustomed to. Statistics show that the average person who has been unemployed since 2008, goes between 18 to 24 months without finding a job. And the longer you are without a job, the tougher it is to get one, because many companies, unfortunately, are not willing to hire people who have been unemployed for too long.

Therefore, personal branding becomes even more important. Marketing yourself is a central core competency for managing and sustaining a successful career. As you are rebuilding your career, it's important to empower yourself by creating the right visibility and getting on the online job sites that will allow potential employers to know that you are available—and not only that you have the right skills, but that you are the right candidate.

Many people are just not comfortable talking about themselves or tooting their own horn, but you have to be able to get past that. Women and minorities in particular don't do that well at all. We often think that "My results will speak for themselves." or "My resume will explain all that I've done and all the experience that I have." But we have to be willing to verbalize our accomplishments and get ourselves out there in a visible way so that people know who we are and what we have to offer. **RYW**

The Three "P's" of Personal Branding

If you want to create your own personal brand effectively, the first thing you have to do is Prepare, which I addressed in Chapter 2. The second P is all about Packaging; and the third P is Presentation.

Preparation

Preparation is about understanding and assessing your skills: What are your *strengths*? What are your *weaknesses*? What new *opportunities* do you bring and what *threats* do you need to address? This is what we coin as a SWOT analysis. Preparation is about putting all the pieces together: dusting off your resume; getting a coach or a mentor with whom you can do some mock interviews and practice some of those skills that may have become dormant; or going back to school and acquiring a new skill. Preparation may be learning new things or gaining new knowledge—in fact, that's an important piece of preparation.

Packaging

The second P is packaging, and this really is an important component because you have to be sure about how you present yourself. You must be transparent and present yourself in a way that people really do see your value, your worth, and also your skills. Packaging may come in the form of a website. What do people see when they first come onto your site? What are you telling them about yourself by what they see on your website? Packaging is about how you position yourself on different social media, or the way you introduce yourself at different networking events. It's how you present yourself in your first interview—how you dress and how you accessorize; your body language and your gestures; your energy level; your smile—those are all a part of Packaging and they lead into the next component—Presentation.

Presentation

Presentation includes not only those things we just listed above, but it is what you say and what you do, and how you do it when you have the opportunity to present yourself. The presentation is more than the interview itself and the content of the interview and the questions you answer. The presentation is in what your resume looks like when it's accessed or when you submit it to a particular job. The presentation is in the way you follow up and in the way you talk to others in the organization. So how are you presenting yourself when you're job seeking and rebuilding your career? **RYW**

Draft Your Elevator Speech

Let me cover one more thing about Presentation. It's critical that you have a two- to three-minute elevator speech—some people call it a pitch. You never know whom you may encounter, who has an opportunity or a job, or who knows someone who has a job opportunity. The number one way that people get jobs right now is through people they know—word of mouth and referrals. Getting a job doesn't happen so much from sending out hundreds of resumes. It's not about the number of jobs you're applying for. It really comes down to people having relationships. That's why I use the phrase, "Turn your contacts into contracts." Getting a job comes through reaching out to other people with whom you've come in contact; people with whom you've established a cordial or courteous relationship; people with whom you at least have had some level of interaction so they feel comfortable enough to refer you or tell you about another job.

I can't count the number of e-mails and phone calls I receive from search firms or colleagues calling to see if there's someone I know who might be available or interested or qualified for a certain job. Over the past year I have connected 50 to 75 people to search firms or jobs. I'm constantly posting them in my LinkedIn account; I'm constantly updating my Twitter account or sending out group e-mails to colleagues saying, "Hey, if you know someone who's interested and qualified, here's a great opportunity."

I encourage you, as part of your personal branding, to use the three Ps: Be prepared. Make sure you've put together the right package—both how you present yourself in person and the documents and materials that describe all your skills, your strengths, your experience. Present and market yourself on different social media sites, your website, and through other means of communication. Make sure that your presentation is not just about what you look like or what you say, but how you say it. Make sure that you have a two- to three-minute elevator speech in which you are able to sell yourself. Successful careers come from those people who are able to connect and collaborate and communicate in a very meaningful way—that's how they turn their contacts into contracts.

So, in two to three minutes, be able to tell people, and sell people, brand "You." Tell people who you are, what you can do, and what value you can bring to the organization. You have to be able to do that in a clear, concise, and compelling way that sets you apart from your competitors—all those other people who are applying for the same job. As my mentor said, "It is better to be prepared for an opportunity and never have one, than to have that opportunity and not be prepared." I can't stress enough that you never know whose path you may cross—that one person who can help you change your life and help you rebuild your career. **RYW**

Preparing to Get the Job

Review Your Resume

Now that you've put all those strategies in place, you've started to get your resume out there, and it's been exposed to so many different jobs and recruiters, the next step occurs when you receive that phone call or e-mail that says, "We want to set up an interview with you." Many organizations are now resorting to phone screeners first before they bring you in for a face-to-face. Sometimes they bypass this step and bring you in as a first interview. But phone screeners are trained to do just that—they're going to screen you. They have already seen your resume; they've already assessed you as having the basic qualifications to match the skills and the job. What they're going to be screening for on the phone in 15–30 minutes is the level of professionalism they sense from you; your ability to answer questions clearly and succinctly; and whether or not you would be a good fit for the culture. So it's important that you treat the phone screen as your first face-to-face interview.

Remember: The *Reinvent Yourself Workbook* provides exercises, reflection questions, and personal assessments based on the material presented in this chapter. WHEN YOU SEE THIS SYMBOL **RYW**, IT MEANS THAT THERE IS A CORRESPONDING EXERCISE OR ACTIVITY FOR YOU TO COMPLETE. Working these exercises will help you to better integrate the material and focus your efforts towards reinventing yourself and achieving success in moving to the next level in your life. Visit **www.drshirleydavis.com/store**.

The first thing you want to do to prepare for that face-to-face, or that phone screen, is to review your resume. Know what you've written; be able to explain your job experiences; be able to explain any lengthy time gaps. If you went from one job to another in a short period of time, be able to explain the difference in the time frame? Did it take you a year to find another job? Were you unemployed during that time? Were you off traveling? Were you sick? Whatever the reason, you may be called upon to answer those questions. The other thing you want to be able to explain is if there are short job stints. If you worked at one job for six months, another job for a year, and then you worked at another job for nine months, that's going to throw up a red flag, and questions. Be ready to explain that in a way that helps them to understand and get a real good sense of your situation. We've all experienced those situations where what looks like a lot of job-hopping turns out to be a college student who was working specific part-time jobs while they were in college. That helps the prospective employer understand that this student not only was committed to completing school, but also wanted to work while they were in school. That shows a level of accountability, growth, and development, and certainly the ability to manage multiple tasks and commitments. So these situations are always taken on a case-by-case basis.

The other thing on your resume that you want to be able to identify and address is your successes at each of the jobs where you worked. What were the results? What were your achievements for each of them? Be able to clearly identify things that you learned from each of those jobs and how you delivered results. The questions from the interviewer will address not just what the results were, but "how" you achieved them. And this will lead into how you worked with others. They're going to ask you behavioral questions, which we in human resources call S.T.A.R. questions. S.T.A.R. stands for Situation, Task, Action, and Result. For example, they may ask you, "Please tell me about a situation or a task you were working on that required you to go above and beyond what you were expected to do." Or they might ask about "a situation in which you were working in a team environment on a project that you had never worked on before, and there was a conflict, or perhaps there was someone on the team who wasn't carrying their workload. Tell me what action you took. What was the particular situation? And what was the result? How did it turn out?" You will be asked behavioral interview questions to ascertain both your background and how you handle certain situations. These questions are designed to get away from the hypothetical "what would you do" and to get at "what did you do when you were in this situation."

Engage in Mock Interviews

Another way to prepare for the interview is to review a list of potential interview questions. There is an abundance of them on the Internet. Just Google "behavioral interview questions," or "job interview questions" and you'll find hundreds of questions. Engage in mock interviews. If you're not going through an outplacement agency, spend some time with friends or colleagues or family members who will be able to help you practice and articulate your responses in a clear and concise way. Why do I say concise? I keep saying concise and succinct because you've got to be able to answer each question in two to three minutes or less:

"What did you do?"

"What did you learn?"

"What did you achieve, and why is that important?"

"Why is that going to add value to this organization?"

In this instance use the K.I.S.S. method (keep it simple and succinct). You want to be able to give the interviewer an opportunity to ask a broad array of questions and you want to present a broad array of your experiences and skills. If you've experienced an interview at which the interviewer only got to two or three questions, that may indicate that your answers were too long, that you went on and on and on. Interviewers tend to check out after a minute—and sometimes as soon as 45 seconds. You have to keep your answers clear and tight, and you have to provide specific examples.

Prepare Your Own Questions and Do Your Homework

Not only do you want to get a list of interview questions to practice and study, you also want to come up with a list of thoughtful questions that you want to ask about the job or about the company. This is important. Please do not go to a job interview and not express any interest or concern about the position. The interviewer wants to know that you're interested and that you've done your homework. So visit the company's website. Look at things like their annual report, news releases, and their social media sites, such as their Facebook page. Go to their career site and look at employee testimonials. Visit other Internet sites to find out about the company itself. Some people have been known to go to Twitter or LinkedIn and find employees who work at that company. You can type in the company name and it will bring up employees who work at that company who have a profile on LinkedIn. You may want to reach out to some of them and find out what working at that company is like. The Internet will also bring up media investor relation sites with information about what's been written about the company—if there have been issues with that company such as recent lawsuits or settlements, or if they've experienced major layoffs, or if they are having financial problems. You want to find out as much information as possible so that you can make an informed decision.

You don't necessarily want to take that kind of information into the interview and ask them, "Why is this? And why is that?" "I read about this ..." or "You guys have these kinds of issues." Don't do that. The information you find online should help you decide whether or not this is the kind of company you want to work for. Or it should give you something to ask other employees as you start to explore the company.

Here are some examples of the types of questions that you want to ask the interviewer: "How would employees in the company describe the culture?" "What are the three key challenges that you face at ABC company, and how are you tackling those challenges?" "Given this global competitive workforce, how are you attracting great talent into the organization and helping them to grow and to develop to be successful?" What resources or what programs are in place to ensure that new employees are set up from day one to be able to achieve success?" Whatever questions you ask, only ask two or three because at the end of the interview the recruiter will often ask you, "Do you have questions for me?" Your answer will be "Yes." You do want to ask thoughtful questions that will help you to determine and decide if this job is the right fit for you. **RYW**

Your Face-to-Face Interview

Get There Early

On the day of the interview, it's important that you make the best impression. This starts with getting there ahead of time. It's been said that if you're on time, you're late. Try to arrive at least 15 minutes ahead of your scheduled interview time. Allow time for traffic, getting lost, and trying to find parking. Then, from the very moment you walk into that building you are selling yourself. From the first person you speak to when you sign in—and you never know who you will be speaking to—to the person who comes to get you to take you into the interview room, you are marketing yourself. Your body language is going to be key. (You may want to go back and revisit Chapter 4 on Retooling Your Communication Skills where I discuss making first impressions, because that's an important aspect that plays into any interview.) Remember, body language makes up 55 percent of your communication, and that can make or break the impression the hiring manager, the recruiter, or even the receptionist that greets you has of you.

Sell Yourself

I was working with a client not too long ago who was interviewing for a senior executive position. From the time that person left the hotel and the car service came to pick her up and took her to the interview location to the time she met with the recruiter, she was selling herself. It was interesting that even the driver provided information to the recruiter saying, "You know what? That's a wonderful, wonderful person. I so enjoyed talking to her. She's so cordial. She was very courteous." or "She's a great communicator." Things like that play into the impression you make from the very moment you first have contact with an organization. What if the driver's first impression was, "She is so mean." She complained the entire drive over here." What if he shares that feedback with the receptionist or the hiring manager. It could be a deal breaker if the driver's opinion is valued. Always remember that whomever you're dealing with, whether it's the receptionist on the phone, the driver who transports you from point A to point B, or the elevator attendant—they all have key insights and may be able to provide input about their impression of the candidate who came in for that job.

Listen, Listen, Listen

I can't stress enough that during the interview you must listen appropriately to the questions being asked; that you're able to answer the questions in a clear, considerate, succinct way; that you're providing the right information for the questions being asked; and that you are selling yourself. But do not oversell yourself. Be careful about using too much "I, I, I, I." The interviewer wants to know if you are a team player, if you are focused on helping others, and if you can work in a team environment for an organization that thinks in terms of "we" and "us" versus "I." Finally, be sure to listen for further instructions from the interviewer so that you're clear on next steps and anything on which you need to follow up.

You're the Best Candidate

You want to end the interview not only with the questions you intend to ask, but with why you believe you're the best candidate for the job. This is when your elevator speech comes in. If they ask you if you have anything else or any parting comments, or if they asked you when you first walked into the interview, "Tell me a little bit about yourself," that's when you want to draw on that elevator speech. It's critical that you can sell yourself right from the beginning, in the middle, and all the way to the end. You want to end the interview with a hearty "thank you for your time, for the opportunity, and for your consideration." You want to give a firm handshake, a warm smile, great eye contact, and you want to let them know that you are looking forward to hearing from them soon.

Follow Up!

Now, you've done a great job in the interview. You nailed it. You feel comfortable that you gave them all the information they were looking for. So you go home—and then what? You send a thank-you note within 24 hours to all the people who interviewed you. You may have to call the recruiter who set up the interview to get their e-mail addresses— I've certainly done that in the past. You want to thank them not only for considering you for that job opportunity, but thank them for their time. Let them know that, based on your skills and qualifications, and what you learned about the job during the interview, you still believe you would be the best candidate and the best fit for their organization.

Navigating in Your Organization

Before I end this section on rebuilding your career, I want to address some issues that many of you will have once you get the new job or may have with the job you already have. These issues include how to navigate the organization, how to show up, how to enhance your career, how to get through issues with bad bosses, and how to cope with being overwhelmed and fatigued and sometimes just feeling stuck. I will share success strategies, not only from my own personal experiences, but from numerous people I've coached in the past, from my clients, and from some of the mistakes I've seen them make. I have been coached and mentored by executives who are highly successful in their own career; I have studied them. I received my Ph.D. in organization and business management with a focus on leadership. So I want to share with you what I've seen, heard, read, learned, and experienced. My purpose in sharing these success strategies is to help you take your career to the next level.

Let me start with the issue that I constantly hear from people I coach. It's an issue I've had to deal with throughout my career. If you are working in an organization that has more than two people, there is a hierarchy set up. You have to deal with the issue called corporate politics and the bureaucracy: "How do I navigate the organizational land mines? How do I deal with the corporate politics?" We all have to deal with this at some point in our career with any organization, because different people are at certain levels. They have certain ways of doing things; they have written rules and, more often than not, they have unspoken and unwritten rules. We have to know how to navigate those organizational land mines because we never know who we might step on (or what we might step in) that would blow up and sabotage our career. So it's important to know these things when you're joining a new organization, or going to work for a new boss or in a new division, or taking on a new or different assignment. You need to be asking questions about some of the things that could potentially explode that you don't even know about.

The other useful definition I've heard about company politics is that it's the science of who gets what when and why. That's what organizational politics are—the questions around the cultural norms. What are the practices and behaviors that get rewarded in the organization? What are the personal agendas at play when you're talking about corporate politics? You never know what may be going on behind the scenes when there is a position being pursued. The politics could be over the control of resources. It could be an advancement of individual goals, and not necessarily team or organizational goals. There are personal agendas at work in an organization that we have to be aware of. It doesn't mean that you have to jump right in and start playing the politics game, but it is important that you at least know that these agendas are at work and what the rules are. Even if you take a step back and don't want to play the game, you at least need to be able to ask the question and to understand the rules the organization plays by.

Know the Key Players

This has been one of the keys to my own career success. From early on in my career, and even more deliberately in the latter part of my career, my first 30 to 60 days at a company is about finding out who are the key players in the organization and who are some of the key resisters. In addition to wanting to know the unspoken rules, I also want to know: "What are some of the obstacles and challenges in the corporate culture?" "What are some of the past issues and some of the fights I wouldn't know about?" It's important that you ask these questions early because you want to recognize, be aware, and acknowledge the company politics. Even if you choose not to get caught up in them, you should know who the troublemakers are; who the power struggles are with; and what the previous issues have been. Even though you are not going to get in the middle of it, it helps to be informed about how you need to approach certain people, so when you see things going on, it gives you a frame of reference and a context to work in.

Know the Key Resisters

We all know that there are some people in our organizations who won't play by the rules; they won't play fair. Some of them prefer to play the games; some of them prefer to play politics; and some will act like they're playing the game, but really they're not. Some act like they have your back, and really they don't. Some act like they don't want your job, but really they do. Some act like they are confident when they are actually threatened and intimidated by you or others. These kinds of people are considered "key resisters." A lot of politics are at play, and sometimes that political game means a zero-sum gain. Somebody has to win and somebody has to lose. I prefer to come out with a win-win

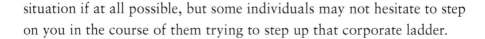

situation if at all possible, but some individuals may not hesitate to step on you in the course of them trying to step up that corporate ladder.

Know How to Deal With Organizational Politics

Organizational politics are important for you to understand—at least how they're played, how they work, and you have to be able to pay close attention. You need to be aware of who's shooting straight and who's playing games—even among those in the senior executive offices. I guarantee you, it's going on at that level, and it's often the reason why you're seeing it at the lower levels, because it starts at the top and then starts to trickle down. You have to be able to watch what happens, not out of rubbernecking fascination, but in the prudent interest of self-preservation. You need to be able to make sure you're watching out for yourself and for what's in the best interests of the organization as well—but you have to make sure you're watching your back.

Then you have to be able to be what I call "positively neutral." This means that you keep a positive attitude, and you do what you need to do in the organization to be successful, but you always remain neutral. Be careful about who you associate with and who you open up to, who you consider a trusted advisor, who you listen to, and who you hang out with. Those are key decisions you have to make. It's all about the politics, because if you connect or link up with or associate with some of the people in the organization who are known troublemakers or who are known shysters, individuals who have been sabotaging other people's careers or who are just people who don't have a good reputation, guess what? By assimilation, your association will attach your reputation to that person or to those people. So be careful about whom you choose to be with and who is in your inner circle.

There are some individuals in your company with whom you get along. There are some who just rub you the wrong way. There are some to whom you simply have to be cordial. And then there are some with whom you need to sit down and have a conversation, because there may be issues and concerns that if you don't address could end up derailing your career. For example, you may have someone in your company who tells you that they're going to work with you on a particular project. Then they don't work with you closely; or they don't work with you fairly; or perhaps they just don't do what they're supposed to do. Sometimes you get a project, and you get people who nod their heads and say they're going to do something, they're going to be at the meeting, they're going to deliver on this result, they're going to send you the information you need, but, quite frankly, you can hardly get them to respond to you. You have to always be open to having that conversation and holding people accountable, but you also have to be able to speak to them in a way that preserves their self-esteem and hopefully your professional relationship. **RYW**

An Example of Navigating the Politics

Here's an example of how I had to navigate some organizational politics and still accomplish a task that was delegated to me. A number of years back, I was asked to put together a strategy to help the company respond to some employee issues and complaints and to figure out ways we could create better employee engagement and job satisfaction. I was asked to put together a particular strategy that wasn't popular in the organization. I needed to find out who in the organization would support it, but also who would be my resisters. I set up a 30- to 45-minute meet-and-greet with all the senior leaders who reported to the president and the CEO. I took some of them out to lunch—even some of the resisters, because I knew who some of them were. Many of these individuals may not have had the opportunity to interact with me had I not invited them out. I wanted to find out what these leaders had in mind for the strategy and what their issues or concerns were. I also wanted to get to know them and for them to get to know me.

During lunch, we had a chance to talk and get to know each other, and I asked them certain targeted questions about putting together the strategy. "What would you do if you were in my position?" I asked. "What are some of the key challenges and obstacles that you believe we would face? What have been some of the start-and-stop measures in the past? Why didn't they work? What did you learn from them?" I asked them, if they were in my position and had this particular role, what would be some of the low-hanging fruit they would go after immediately. I asked them these kinds of targeted questions to help inform the strategy I knew I had to develop. I was also keen enough to know that I didn't want to have a strategy that only had Shirley's name on it and that they would feel I was pushing on to them because I had not included or at least solicited their input. I wanted this to be presented as "our" strategy.

Once I got all the input from all these leaders, I pulled together a strategy that incorporated the feedback they had shared with me—good, bad, and indifferent. I included the common themes, and I had some outliers; but I made sure that the input of those who were the biggest champions and advocates of this strategy was heard. Moreover, I included input from those who I knew were resisters.

I went back to the president and asked him if I could insinuate myself onto his next leadership meeting agenda and propose this strategy. It's important, as I talk about organizational politics, to note that I was galvanizing the group of leaders in the organization to embrace a strategy that many of them had questions about and didn't really want. This particular strategy was on how to better engage employees, how to ensure that all employees had equal access to opportunities, that we posted certain jobs and everyone was aware of them, and that the appropriate coaching/feedback was provided.

When I got on the president's agenda, I knew from the corporate politics perspective that I had to present this as "our" strategy. I had to continue to reiterate that this was something each and every one of them contributed to part by part. As I went around the room on the day of the meeting, I thanked each one of them for their input. I wanted to make it clear that I had met with all their peers and colleagues in the room. I said things like, "When I met with John, for example, John shared with me this really great idea that I recommend we incorporate." Or I said,

"When I was meeting with Susan, she shared some issues with me that were obstacles we needed to consider if we implemented this kind of a solution." And I said, "Hey, Pete, you mentioned that you shared a few considerations for the timeline based on some major projects that we would be launching and I've incorporated them into this strategy." Sometimes what you have to do as you're navigating these land mines and resistance is to put it out there in a very politically savvy way, and make it be a part of everyone's input and not just your own.

As I'm calling out the names of the president's direct reports right there in front of the group, highlighting their great ideas and thanking them for their input, I'm demonstrating to the president that the creation of the strategy was a collaborative effort. How many of those leaders in the room do you really think were going to come out and say, "Well, no, I don't agree with this strategy," or "No, I'm against growing our talent and making sure that we're administering our policies for our employees in a consistent way." That wasn't going to happen. I was able to present it in a way that made each of them look involved, engaged, and committed, and it made me look like a collaborative team player. The fact is, I genuinely did want to know how they felt. I wanted their input, and I needed their support in order to create the best strategy.

This is just one example of how I navigated the organizational politics, got a win-win outcome, and and increased my profile as a credible leader. You have to make sure that you are inclusive, strategic, and that you are getting the input of many different people. People want to feel that they are a part of something, or that you're collaborating with them by reaching out and seeking their insights and expertise. And this was one way of doing so within the organizational context.

What is the Organization's Perception of You?

Another strategy for navigating organizational politics is to proactively seek coaching and feedback on how people perceive you in the organization. Whether you get that from your boss, your team members, your direct reports, or some of your close colleagues and friends, this kind of feedback is critical. You want to know how you're perceived on different projects, in different teams, and in different assignments.

The thing about feedback is that everybody has an opinion, and you don't want to trust everybody's opinion. Use the one rule that I've used: "Learn how to eat the meat and spit out the bones." And don't take it personally. People will say some things to you that make sense and that apply to you; then there are going to be things that just don't resonate with you, that don't align with your values—it just isn't you at all. You have to learn how to decipher which things really apply and which things come out of left field.

With corporate politics you don't want to isolate yourself in your organization. Often, we tend to go into our little corner, into our office or cubicle, and work on our own. In reality, we're isolating ourselves and sending a very real message that we don't want to be engaged or that we're not a team player. You may be working on a very important project, but you still have to take a break at some point, walk down the hallway or be in the meetings you need to be in, and not isolate yourself—get out and talk to people; get to know people. **RYW**

Find Allies in the Organization

The last strategy for navigating organizational land mines or corporate politics is to find allies in the organization and use your allies as champions; let them influence your resisters and your naysayers. In the example I used earlier for how I went about building an inclusion strategy, I knew that there were some people who were just not going to support it; they were going to poke holes in it. But I used a very strategic tactic: I brought them to the table and engaged them in a way that the strategy did make sense—that it was incorporating their input and feedback. Most people aren't going to shoot down their own ideas.

When you have enough of the people as your champions and your advocates, let them be the ones to call their peers on the carpet. It's probably career suicide for you to challenge someone who is at a higher level than you, especially to challenge them publicly in front of their peers. So I would caution you to be very careful about how you push back, because that's how they view challenging their opinions or calling them out and stating outright that they're wrong. Handle that situation in a more savvy and a more professional way that maintains the relationship and also preserves their self-esteem. **RYW**

Bad Boss, Good Boss

The next area to address is how to deal with a bad boss, and hopefully you're not this person or working for this person, although most likely you have at some point in your career. I've had to deal with many bad bosses in my life. I have probably had more average, mediocre, or bad bosses than I've had good bosses. The good news is that over the last ten years of my career, I've had really good bosses. Early on in my career, however, I had a couple of bad bosses who left an indelible impression on me—they taught me how NOT to be when I became a leader or supervisor or people manager.

If you have a bad boss, it's going to be difficult for you to change them. There are some things you have to do in order to be able to tolerate them or to be able to work with them without ticking them off further. One is to have some early upfront conversations with them about what is important to you in a leader and how best you can work together. You might even talk about your own leadership style; address what you need in the way of development and coaching, and how often you need it. It may involve setting up specific meetings, getting on a schedule where you can talk about your progress, your results, your career paths, and where you can solicit their feedback and make requests and even tell them where you need additional support and coaching. You may want to talk about your expectations or their expectations of you. Ask them, "What does success look like?" "What does 'meets expectations' or 'exceeds expectations' look like on the performance-rating continuum?" And ask frequently how you're doing. You want to check in with them, give them reports or status updates on where your projects and assignments are—you just want to be proactive. From a corporate politics standpoint, it doesn't hurt to give them some public acknowledgment for their support, especially when they've been instrumental in helping you to succeed.

Bad bosses don't often do that, but these are steps you can take at least to initiate a cordial working relationship. There are reasons why bad bosses are the way they are. Sometimes they had a bad boss; that's the model they had and they don't know any different. There are bad bosses who are insecure and threatened because they have a lack of skills or competencies or experience. Some bosses didn't get their job based on merit; they got it because of who they knew, or even because of other reasons. They may not even know their own blind spots and have never received coaching, direction or feedback; nor have they ever been told that their management style is ineffective.

Strategies for Dealing With a Bad Boss

I'm not saying that it becomes your job to let them know they're a bad boss, but I am saying that it's still your responsibility to deal with the situation. You want to make sure that you're successful at your job and that you can at least work with the boss you've got until you can make other changes and other arrangements. Obviously, if you have a bad boss who is sabotaging you, giving you ratings that are unmerited, and stealing all the credit for your great ideas, you have to deal with all these things accordingly. There are ways to do this. It may be by having a conversation with them about the idea you shared and that they didn't give you credit when they mentioned it in another meeting. It may be by having a conversation about getting more feedback—that you would like to have feedback so that you know how well you're doing or what you need to work on. It might be that you feel like the boss is demeaning you or saying things about you publicly that are disrespectful, untrue, or even harassing. In this case, you need to have a conversation with the HR manager to ensure that a complaint is lodged and handled appropriately.

There are also anonymous ways to handle bad bosses. Some organizations have suggestion boxes or 360-degree feedback during performance review times when you're able to provide feedback to your boss's boss. There may even be occasions when you go and have a private one-on-one conversation with your boss's boss and let them know some of the issues—and you may have to document that. You may want to keep a record, or at least know the dates and times and specific examples of when things happened, so that you'll be able to recall the details. I do hope that you're not working in that kind of hostile situation, because that really crosses the line into violating laws around creating hostile environments for workers. These are some of the ways you can take ownership of your own career and at least try to have a working and cordial relationship with your manager. **RYW**

Managing Your Own Career

Take Calculated Risks

I have a couple of other tips for you to incorporate as you rebuild your career. I always tell people to make sure that they are managing their own ability to take risks, and I mean calculated risks. Many people work in organizations or companies that are fairly risk averse. They don't like to challenge the status quo; they don't want to make waves. They don't want to do new things or think way outside the box because, as they say, if it's working people don't want to change it—don't fix it if it's not broken. You may want to be innovative, do different things, and try new approaches that may be more efficient, more profitable and economical. So you have to be willing to take risks. Even if the organization is risk averse, you have to be willing to take personal calculated risks for your own development, to grow and learn new skills. This is an important part of your own ability to rebuild and to continue to update and upgrade your own resume. This would be a great opportunity to engage your advocate or mentor in the organization to bounce new ideas off them. And, if you have a good relationship with your direct supervisor, they can be a great resource to solicit feedback on your ideas as well. They can also support you in getting your ideas implemented.

Taking calculated risks may mean doing some things that you've never done before, such as taking on new assignments. It may be offering to participate on new project assignments or taking on stretch roles that will help you grow and develop. It may be mentoring, or partnering, or getting a peer coach to learn new skills in a different area. It may be agreeing to take a new course or to attend a session your employer is offering that you haven't taken before. All of these are designed to increase your learning, because you have to be a life-long learner and a student of the organization—that's really important if you want to continue to increase your value.

Move Outside Your Comfort Zone

One of the greatest career opportunities I had, and it was a turning point in my career, was that I took on a role outside of human resources even though I had been working seven or eight years in that field. I was housed in HR in what was jokingly referred to by employees as "the ivory tower." Their perception was that HR was in this big building where all the decisions were made and then rolled out to the rest of the organization. We created policies and mandatory training programs that all employees had to attend. And we were rigid, out of touch, and employer-focused (versus employee-focused). That's the way they perceived us. One day I got an offer from a colleague of mine who called and asked if I'd be interested in heading up their training and development in the operations side of the business. Well, I had never left the ivory tower, and I had never separated myself from the corporate headquarters. In this new position, I was not going to be working in the HR department anymore.

I gave it some thought and I realized that I needed to learn the business. I needed to be able to relate better to the operations managers, the supervisors, the front line leaders, those who were making the money, those who were working with our customers and dealing with customer complaints, and those were helping us to produce the widgets and the products. I was a little reluctant at first, but only because it was outside my comfort zone. It was something new and different, but I decided that I was going to take on this role. It was probably the game changer for me that catapulted me to greater success later in my career, because once I got over into the operations group, I started to learn the language of business. I had an opportunity to be on the front line, to see how we made products, how we interfaced with and serviced our customers, how we generated revenue, how we increased our market share, and how we created our marketing and our branding strategies.

It gave me a broader exposure to the rest of the organization and taught me the business side, and had I not done that, I wouldn't be able to walk into the C suite today and talk the language of business—about profit share, stock price growth, product innovation, customer interactions, and quality process improvement. I wouldn't know how we increased efficiencies on the front line, and how we minimized the bottlenecks blocking us from being more efficient at creating widgets in a much faster, more economical way.

By learning that language, I was able to make better offers to my clients by speaking their language. I was able to shift and change the way I implemented my strategies. I was no longer mandating training that everyone had to attend but couldn't see the value in. And I was able to understand that they were working in a 24-hour, seven-day-a-week operation, so taking them off the floor was taking money out of their pockets and impacting their ability to be more productive. By working on the front line like that and getting a sense of what they really needed and how the operations worked, I was able to shift my paradigm and come up with strategies that helped them to decrease the ramp-up time for new hires, to produce widgets in a faster manner, and to create better quality products.

Those shifts and those changes really helped me. Today I am back in the HR group, in the ivory tower if you will, and I'm able to create strategies that I know will be embraced by operations. I'm able to talk in language they understand so that when I go to them and make specific requests that I need them to deliver on, I can ask in such a way that I show the value proposition and how it benefits them, and how it's going to benefit the organization at large. So it was a great experience for me to take that kind of risk, and I'm glad I did because it gave me new skills and exposed me to a broader context of the organization that I would not have had, had I not taken that calculated risk.

Choose Your Battles

You shouldn't have a problem with every single person and with everything in the organization. Not everything is wrong in organizations. If you've got a problem everywhere you go and with every company you work for and everybody you work with, then, I must say, it may not be the company—it may not be them if you are the common denominator. It may be you. You have to be optimistic, and you have to seize opportunities where you can grow and develop and change versus constantly trying to change everything else around you.

As you read these tips and strategies and tools that I'm giving you to use and implement, I hope that you take them seriously. Take advantage of all the resources and all the benefits that are available to you, through your organization, through your peers, through your community, and even at home. It's important that you take care of yourself. It's important that you look out for your best interests, because at the end of the day you have to make sure that you've got the health, the wellness, the strength, and the peace of mind to be able to get done what you need to get done. You can't reinvent your career if you first don't reinvent yourself. So take good care of yourself and make sure that you're executing all these strategies and taking responsibility for your own development.

Summary

- Think about the changes in the workplace, the number of women in the workforce, the rapidly changing world of technology, and the tight job situation.

- Now is the time to consider how to rebuild our career in the midst of these workforce shifts and changing circumstances, how to embrace the changes and not be paralyzed by them.
- The six steps toward rebuilding your career include: embracing change, avoiding pity parties, getting better not bitter, turning contacts into contracts, inventorying your strengths and skills, and reestablishing your personal brand.
- To create your own personal brand effectively, you need to take the necessary steps in the way of Preparation, Packaging, and Presentation—the Three "P's."
- Your elevator speech should allow you to say who you are, how you're qualified, and why you're the best person for the job in two minutes or less.
- Go over your interview checklist and prepare yourself by asking all the right questions before the interview, be ready for your screening and the interview itself, and most importantly, follow up.
- Once you get the job, or if you already have the job, you will face issues over how to navigate the organizational politics. Some examples include: knowing the key players and how to leverage them, knowing the key resisters and how to engage them, knowing the perception that the organizational leaders have of you, and knowing how to deal with a bad boss.
- Three tips for managing your own career: take calculated risks, move outside your comfort zone, and choose your battles.

CHAPTER SIX:
Reevaluating Your Relationships

Relationship Assessment

DO YOU HAVE HEALTHY AND HAPPY RELATIONSHIPS? Are they nurturing relationships? Do you have people around you who build you up, who speak to your life, and who strengthen you? If you do, how are you leveraging and utilizing those relationships to help you become better?

Or, conversely, do you have people around you who are toxic people—people who are always trying to tear you down, who speak negative things and give off negative vibes and energy into your life, and who really don't have your back? If you do, why is this the case? Why do you have toxic people in your life? Are you attracting toxic people? Why have you chosen to keep them in your life as long as you have? And, when you're ready, how do you get rid of the toxic people in your life?

In the very first chapter I addressed self-esteem and the fact that self-image derailers often come in the form of NIOPs: the negative influences of other people. I know it's human nature that we tend to be more negative than we are positive or that we tend to complain more than we compliment. We even tend to see the glass half-empty versus half-full. Most Americans tend to fall into the first category. But you don't have to. If you work toward your purpose, and you set goals for yourself, and you walk through the exercises and activities that I am laying out for you, you can reinvent yourself. And when you know who you are, why you were created, and you have set a plan for accomplishing that, you will be stepping into your greatness. You don't have to settle for the glass half-full. You should be striving to live a life where the glass is not only full, but overflowing.

Isn't that a powerful question to reflect and ponder over? My coach, friend, and mentor, Mr. Les Brown, who I referenced earlier, made a powerful statement to me years ago, and it really impacted my life. He said: "Shirley, if you show me your five closest friends, I'll show you your future. I'll show you the likelihood of you achieving success and the likelihood of you stepping into your greatness and projecting a strong sense of self-worth." Here's his thought: If you're the smartest person in your group, you have to find a new set of friends or at least expand your inner circle of friends. If you have people who are smarter than you or at least going in the same direction as far as your values, your goals, your ambitions, your drive, and your dreams are concerned, those people will stretch you. You will learn from them; you'll help each other get where you want to go. There's an old proverb that says, "Iron sharpens iron." You will develop one another and challenge each other—and that's a good thing. So, whoever you choose to stay inside your circle will have a lot to do with your future success or lack thereof. List your five closest friends. Now, review that list and identify or categorize those five relationships according to their healthy, wholesome influence. Are there any who are unhealthy or even toxic?

Toxic Relationships

How do you know if you're in a toxic relationship or if you have a toxic person around you? You will know because toxic people will betray

Remember: The *Reinvent Yourself Workbook* provides exercises, reflection questions, and personal assessments based on the material presented in this chapter. WHEN YOU SEE THIS SYMBOL **RYW**, IT MEANS THAT THERE IS A CORRESPONDING EXERCISE OR ACTIVITY FOR YOU TO COMPLETE. Working these exercises will help you to better integrate the material and focus your efforts towards reinventing yourself and achieving success in moving to the next level in your life. Visit **www.drshirleydavis.com/store**.

you. They'll abuse you; they become co-dependent; they often become a crutch to you. These are people who have ongoing drama or too much baggage in their lives. They don't build you up, but they often tear you down or bring you down to their level. They don't dream big. They only see the glass half-empty, and sometimes completely empty. These are people who remember who you were back in the day. They continue to rehash those things, even when you try to think bigger or better or try to improve your life. They remember you when. These are people who are the voice of nonreason who always say, "Well, you can't do that." "You aren't able." "You don't have the ability to do that." "I don't understand why you're even thinking that way." Those individuals are not there to help you take your life to the next level. They are that negative influence in your life that can't see you moving beyond where you are right now. These people can't seem to keep a job; they don't have any commitment to anything; they are constantly looking for the downside.

Let me stop there. Do you have people in your life who fit this bill? They are destructive. They are the NIOPs: the negative influences of other people. You have to look at each relationship in your life and ask: "What is this relationship doing FOR me?" "What is this relationship doing TO me?" "What is it doing to me if it's not building me up, helping me grow spiritually, financially, intellectually, personally, emotionally, or even helping me to become a better person?" **RYW**

Why Do You Keep Toxic People in Your Life?

Now that you have identified your list and categorized them as healthy and wholesome or put them in the toxic category, ask yourself, "Then why do I allow toxic people to stay in my life?" "What is it that I'm doing or what energy or what aura am I putting out that continues to attract toxic people?" Sometimes we can attract people who are similar to ourselves; the energy we put out is like a magnet that attracts other people just like us.

I did not pose the question whether or not you were a toxic person yourself. I hope that you have done a self-assessment. If you feel like you are one of those toxic people I described above, then you have a lot more work to do. But as we focus on your inner circle, it's important that you identify any predators, or people who are out to destroy your destiny or who are really not friends. They're "frenemies," because they're capitalizing on your vulnerabilities and your weaknesses and they undermine and sabotage God's purpose in your life, and in the end they ruin you. By the time they leave, you've lost everything. They've ruined your mental state and your physical health and well-being; you're emotionally distraught; you're financially unstable. Sometimes we tend to keep these people in our lives because we think we can rehabilitate them. If you think you're going to be able to change someone else who's an adult or a grown person, or, frankly, another human being, the answer is—you won't. You have to focus on you. It's a full-time job trying to change yourself. You have to focus on yourself first and not try to change other people.

People who are toxic by nature tend to sting you. Have you ever heard the story of the scorpion and the tortoise? The scorpion wanted to get to the other side of the river. The scorpion saw the turtle going across the river and said to the turtle, "Hey, I'd love to get a ride across the river to the other side. Can I ride with you?" The tortoise said, "No, you will sting me." The scorpion promised and committed: "No, no, no. I just want to ride over to the other side of the river. I promise I won't sting you. I promise, I promise!" The tortoise said, "No. I know you're saying that you won't, but I just know that you will, because that's what you know to do." The scorpion continued and insisted that it was not going to sting the tortoise and continued to beg and plead and ask the tortoise to take him across on his back. Finally, the tortoise gave in and just as he was about to reach the other side of the river, guess what! The scorpion stung him. The tortoise said to the scorpion, "Hey, you said you weren't going to do this. You promised me. You committed to me that you would not sting me." And the scorpion said to the tortoise, "That's my nature."

You have to be able to distinguish between those who will sting you because it's their nature and those who have your best interests at heart and mean you well. Having had these relationships in my life, I have learned how to spot them from a mile away, how to deal with them, and how to unapologetically be selective about who I allow in my inner circle. I have developed this intolerance for people with drama and baggage. I break out into hives. It makes me itch. It gives me the heebie-jeebies. What about you? You have to develop a predator detector, a toxic person radar. You have to figure out how to eliminate the toxic people in your life, how to continue making right decisions and attract the right kind of people in the future.

There are ways you can cope with toxic people. Every time you have a toxic person in your life doesn't mean that you have to get rid of them; there may be other strategies and other solutions. Let's address those now. **RYW**

Strategies for Coping with Toxic People

Toxic people are everywhere. We can all name at least one toxic person we've run across in our life, whether in our home, our community, our workplace, or, unfortunately, even in our place of worship. Those people in our lives who become a part of our inner circle are the people who have the greatest impact on us. But if you have identified someone who's toxic in your life, it doesn't mean that you have to throw the baby out with the bath water. Consider the following strategies.

Confrontation

One recommendation I would make is to confront them and give them a chance to make changes. Remember, we can't change grown people, but there's nothing wrong with giving them an opportunity to make the changes themselves. You may want to have a conversation with them or send them a letter, or whatever you feel comfortable doing, to let them know why you're not happy in the relationship or that you feel their actions or behaviors or attitude toward you is hurting the relationship.

It could be that they are oblivious to their behavior. If they're good people and they mean you well and they value the relationship, they will adjust accordingly. At the very least, you may be able to understand why they're doing what they're doing or what's driving them, or the rationale behind their behavior, and you may be able to help them address it themselves and become a support to them.

Elimination

Unfortunately, what usually happens is that there's a clash of expectations, personalities, and understanding that leads to relationships becoming even more toxic. No amount of moaning will fix them and you may have to move on to the next stage. My recommendation for this kind of toxic situation is to cut them off completely and distance yourself. This takes courage, especially if it's a relationship you've been invested in and involved in for quite a while, but you have to know when the liabilities outweigh the assets. You have to have the willingness to correct or compromise or communicate, and if they have no willingness at all, then you have to be willing to cut the relationship off for your own survival.

Cutting the relationship off doesn't mean killing the person. It doesn't mean making it a personal battle. It doesn't even mean assassinating the other person's character. If matching their attitude to the relationship doesn't work, then you're best off just cutting them out of your life as much as possible. While it's not practical to go so far as to get a new job or relocate just to avoid somebody, don't think that simply cutting someone off or cutting ties with them is going to change the situation. You have to determine what's going to work best to help you keep peace, continue to move forward and be positive, and accomplish what you need to accomplish.

If that toxic person remains toxic and tries to continue the same relationship with you, then you have to take a bold step and be much clearer about cutting off the connection. This may mean blocking them totally by deleting their e-mail address, deleting them from your phone, removing them from your Facebook page, blocking them from any other social media contacts. Remember, your happiness is paramount, so don't let self-obsessed or negative people ruin yours.

When You Have No Choice

What if you have to work with toxic people? You have to go to work every day. Obviously you don't want to quit your job and relocate somewhere else to remove them from your life, but there are a couple of ways to deal with them in the workplace. First of all, don't take it personally. This kind of toxic person is probably toxic with everybody else too. They are an equal opportunity predator and it's their problem, not yours. Consider the source and let it go.

Second, I recommend that you keep your self-esteem intact. A strong sense of self-esteem can help you to detract some of the toxic behaviors that this person may spew your way. Believe in yourself; stick to your purpose; hold fast to your sense of self-worth; and never let anybody have that much power and control over you that you allow them to sabotage your destiny. Third, I suggest that you pick your battles. Some battles are worth fighting and others are not. There are some hills that you just don't want to die on. You will achieve your own personal victory by knowing the difference and knowing when to avoid it and when to cut it off. Don't try to do everything; don't try to please everyone. It is not going to benefit you at all, and it would be a waste of your energy and your time.

Take Care of Yourself

In a way, you need to be selfish. If you suffer burnout, physical problems, or mental problems as a result of a toxic person, it's you who will ultimately deal with the fallout, not him or her. So take care of yourself. This means that you may want to reach out and solicit the help of those who are your closest friends—those healthy, wholesome friends on your list. Toxic people are stressful; they will wear you down. Your reaction to stress can prevent you from thinking clearly and objectively, so it's important sometimes to have someone with a more objective viewpoint who can help you cope with the situation. Ask a friend, a spouse or a respected business colleague, but don't go to the other people in the workplace. And, if you ask for help, it's not a sign of weakness but a sign of strength.

If this person becomes too toxic at work—and we're talking here of crossing the line of harassment and creating a hostile environment—now you're getting into a legal issue where you have to report it to your human resources department. Never allow someone in your workplace to be toxic, to sabotage or disrespect you to the degree that it crosses the line of becoming hostile. It's wrong.

Pray for Them
My last recommendation is that you also pray for them. This should be the first line of defense and also the last resort. Remember, you can't manage anybody else's attitude or basic happiness; just take care of your own. People will do to you what you allow them to do to you, so you have to develop boundaries for what you will allow in your life, and what you won't allow, and you have to stand your ground.

To recap: If you have toxic people in your life, you don't necessarily have to immediately cut them off. You can have a conversation and confront them and give them an opportunity to change. If they do, and the relationship turns around, and it becomes a positive, healthy relationship, that's great. If it does not, then you have to decide whether to cut the relationship off, distance yourself, or disassociate from that person and move forward. Build other relationships and continue to be selective. **RYW**

Nurturing Relationships
Let's address nurturing relationships. We've addressed negativity enough; you've got the point. Let's look into the benefits of having people around you who are nurturing, who are healthy, and who are helping you. Again, nurturing relationships are going to bring out the

best in you; they're going to keep you focused; they're going to build you up and make you stronger. Having healthy people around you will drive you to be better. There are people who may even help you take advantage of new opportunities and open new doors. They may encourage you to go back to school, to take classes, to pursue a certification. They will inspire you. They'll have a positive attitude. They'll understand who you are. They may even help you in job situations, perhaps connect you to other great people who might be able to open certain doors for you. These are people who are productive. These are the kinds of people that you want to have in your life because they are going to speak positive energy into your life. They are going with you on the journey toward greatness.

The Three Foot Rule

Remember that three foot rule. When you come within three feet of someone else, either there is a blessing you have for them or there is a blessing they have to give to you. This illustrates the importance of having that inner circle; the people that you trust; people who are privy to information about you that no one else is; and people that you seek as part of your "dream team." You want them to help build your dream, not steal it. And you have to have several key people around you because you can't get everything from any one person—no one is going to be everything to you. If you're looking for that, you will always be disappointed. Your needs are too varied and too vast. Don't do this to your spouse or significant other; don't do this to your children or to your family, to your business partner or anyone else. You have to have other sources around you. No one person can be the end all and be all of everything you need. Don't ask your inner circle for things they can't do; but find out what they can do and be content with that.

When you don't have other friends in your life than your spouse, you are putting too much pressure on him or her to be everything you need; they were not created to be your everything. Only your God can do that. It's a mistake that a lot of people make, even on their jobs. They try to get all their financial needs met through one job, and that will never work. You have to create multiple streams of income, whether it's through an investment, a business on the side, or whatever it may be, but you cannot rely on one thing to be your sole source of support. That's why networking is so important.

The Six Types of Relationships

Networking is all about creating relationships, so let's talk about the different kinds of relationships we should have. There are relationships other than your inner circle of your friends, or those five closest relationships on your list, but let's address the different types of relationships that you want to develop and nurture in your life. We experience a variety of relationships throughout our lifetime—some we have a choice in and others we have no control over at all. For example, we didn't get to pick our parents or our brothers and sisters; we were born into our family. But we can be selective about other relationships. Obviously, we want to have different kinds of people in our lives for different reasons; circumstances dictate that at different stages and ages in our life. I believe there are six kinds of relationships we'll have over our lifetime. I'll address each kind in detail: **RYW**

1. Personal relationships
2. Effective mentoring relationships
3. Authoritative relationships
4. Key business contacts or professional associations
5. Alliances and partnerships
6. Advocates, champions, or sponsors

1. Personal Relationships

The first type consists of personal relationships, which I'm not going to go into in much detail because we've already discussed personal relationships at length. As I mentioned above, we don't get to choose family members and the children God gives to us. Yes, we get to choose when we become foster parents or when we adopt children, but when we're birthing children, we don't get to choose what God gives us; and we don't get to choose all their features and unique characteristics.

The other personal relationships in our lives we get to choose, such as our spouse or our partner or significant other, our best friends and other close friends—we do have a hand in choosing these. These are the people who will help shape and mold and develop us for the future; they will have a direct impact on our values, our character, our beliefs, and our habits; ultimately they will even inform our decisions. These are people who have access to and are privy to our personal and private lives to some degree; we trust these people. These are people we can confide in and seek out their advice and hopefully listen to; these are people who know our strengths and our weaknesses—and they knew us back when. It's important to have personal relationships, but you know what they always say: Sometimes those who are closest to you can hurt you the most. But they can also be a great blessing in your life. So be very selective about the people you choose to have in your inner circle. **RYW**

2. Mentors

The second type of relationship is the effective mentoring relationship. These are usually informal relationships with people who help you grow and develop in your career or in your professional life for a specific reason. It might be to enhance your promotability at work, for instance, or in a business. It might be to help you leverage a relationship. It might be to build your leadership skills and credibility. You might have a mentor who helps you increase your professional effectiveness, your communication or presentation skills, your ability to influence and nego-tiate. Your mentoring may be learning from those who already have the skills, who've been there, done that, and have a certain level of success under their belt. No one selects a mentor who is less capable or qualified than they are. We seek out people whom we admire and respect; who have certain skills and strengths; and who have accomplished a level of credibility and success in the workplace. These are people we want to emulate or model. Mentoring relationships are a means to an end. The most successful people I know and whose biographies I have read in business journals all admit that they had a mentor along the way and that it was a key ingredient to their rise to success.

So write down the names of those you consider to be your mentors. Now, think about why you selected those people as mentors. What are some of the skills and characteristics and strengths that you saw in them and admired? What level of success have you achieved so far by having those people in your life? Next, think about how you're leveraging those relationships, how you're capitalizing on their level of success and on the skills and expertise they have. You don't want to have a mentor just to say you have a mentor; there is always a reason for having one. A mentor is a means to an end.

Having a mentor is not just about getting something from someone else. Being in a mentoring relationship could become a mutual mentoring situation or a kind of reverse mentoring situation. What this means is that not only is your mentor sowing seeds in your life, providing good coaching, giving you expertise, and helping you to develop skills and strengths, but it means that you're also able to provide perspective for the mentor. The mentor may come out of the relationship with a better understanding of some things that you've been challenged with, or of things going on in the organization unknown to the mentor. You may be able to enlighten him or her about certain areas of the workplace that he or she might be able to influence or change, or about specific areas where there might be discrimination or oversight where people are just not paying attention. The relationship can become a mutual mentoring situation (or what is also referred to as reverse mentoring).

I remember selecting my mentors, and the key word is "selecting." You have to be very clear about what you want to accomplish and what this person can bring to the relationship. I also remember being able to share with my mentors how I saw things, and how I viewed the world. And coming from me, especially from someone at a lower level in the organization seeking a person at the senior or executive level, they're able to hear a perspective from someone a couple of levels down. They don't always necessarily get to hear that, so reverse mentoring can be an effective win-win for both of you. **RYW**

3. Authoritative Relationships

The third type of relationship involves a leadership role, having a boss or a leader. I prefer to use the term "employee-employer" relationship or "direct report" versus the term "subordinate." This is a relationship between one who has direct leadership and authority over you, whether it's in the workplace, in a community setting, at church, or in civic activities. These are the people around you, such as your boss or the leader of a team project that you're working on, or the director of an organization you volunteer for. It could be your pastor/priest/spiritual leader. It could be the head of the board of directors that you're on. It could be your teacher or the head of a university or school that you attend.

It's important that you have a good relationship with those who have authority because they're the ones who are leading and guiding you, providing you direction, giving you coaching, and even offering feedback. They have a direct impact over your career and your promotability or over your pay and upward mobility in an organization. Make sure that you cultivate these relationships; work to keep them healthy and wholesome. These are relationships in which you have a say in how they're shaped and formed, because you have a part to play in ensuring that these relationships are working.

I can't say enough about the importance of having a good relationship with those who have authority over you, because if you've had a bad boss—and I know many of us have—these are people who can have a lasting effect on your career. It affects whether or not you even want to come to work, your level of productivity, engagement, and your ability to be creative. Statistics show that nearly 56 percent of people in the workplace are miserable on their jobs. They're not very engaged, they're not very committed; they do just enough not to get fired, and they're getting paid just enough not to quit. I tell organizational leaders all the time, "You have to do a better job of building a great place to work and being an employer of choice, and even being a leader in the 21st century. You have to be a leader of choice because you are losing a lot of money and productivity because people are coming to work and are not giving 100 percent and are not being fully utilized." There are multiple billions of dollars lost each year because of low productivity due to morale issues, low satisfaction, and low engagement.

I got the opportunity to work with one of the best bosses I've ever had for almost six years. I built a great relationship with him. He was smart, intelligent, personable, and worldly. By "worldly" I mean that he had lived around the world; he had lots of experiences and he was willing to share them. He was also quite well read. I think he read a book or two a week. He was constantly sharing statistics and history facts and great stories and issues he came across, and he was able to deal with them and address them in the organization. He was a champion for me. He gave me a lot of great feedback, allowed me the opportunity to grow and to learn, trusted me as an expert in what I was doing, and allowed me the autonomy to be able to make my own decisions—he provided me great coaching and direction.

That's the kind of relationship I still enjoy because, even though he's moved on to bigger and better things, we stay in touch with each other. I still consider him a coach and a friend, and he is still able to connect me with the right people or help me to think through how to solve certain problems or deal with certain issues. These are the kinds of employee-employer relationships you can build, and they can be relationships that have an impact on you across the organization, externally with clients, customers, and other colleagues, and in your personal life.

Now I've covered the first three types of relationships: personal relationships, mentoring relationships and boss-to-employee relationships. It's important to remember that you cannot be successful in your life if you don't successfully leverage and capitalize on the relationships and the people who cross your path. Remember, these are people for whom, if they come within three feet of you, have a blessing for you or you have one for them. I often remember the saying, "People come into your life for a reason, a season, or a lifetime." It's important to know why people are coming into your life. They may come into your life for only one reason, for you to gain some knowledge or to learn something new you didn't already know, or to get a referral. Moreover, you may never see that person again. Then there are people who come into your life for a season. They may be there for a short period of time or an extended period of time, but they form a relationship with you for a reason. Then you have people who will be in your life for a lifetime. I've got best friends of 25 years. They came across my path; I capitalized on the relationships, leveraged the contacts, and turned them into lifelong friendships—they are my two best friends; we live on two different sides of the country, yet we stay in touch. I feel just as close to them as I did in our younger years. People will come into your life and you've got to be able to leverage that relationship; you've got to know why they're there: is it for a reason, for a season, or is it for a lifetime? **RYW**

4. Key Business Contacts

The next type of relationship is comprised of those key business contacts and those contacts you make in professional associations. These are people you meet in the community or in a business setting or in your day-to-day activities who have or do something useful for you or for whom you have or do something in return. These relationships have the potential of providing you with a service or a referral, or a discount or product that will ultimately benefit you. And you have the same thing for them. These are relationships that you can leverage; you can "turn contacts into contracts" or "leverage your network and turn it into net worth."

Do you know how to do this? Do you know how to do it effectively? What I've discovered is that not everyone knows how to effectively network and leverage this kind of business relationship or contact. Have you ever been to a conference or a networking event or some kind of a community event, and, as you're exchanging cards and talking, you find that you have some things in common and you vow that you're going to stay connected? "I'll catch up with you. I'll give you a call." And then what happens? You know what happens: we get back to the office and we tuck the business card away in a drawer somewhere or lay it on our desk. We might file it in our Outlook contacts, but often it just gathers dust. We have to learn how to leverage these relationships for a particular purpose. Let me give you an example.

I consider myself a master networker. I build relationships, keep contacts, and really leverage them—I think, in a very positive and effective way. I do that for a living; I'm always gathering business cards. People are always walking up to me and giving me their business cards or asking me for mine, or they're sending me e-mails. I'm constantly getting notifications to be connected on LinkedIn, befriended on Facebook, and followed on Twitter. With the business cards, when I get back to my office I literally put them into my Outlook contacts. When a situation or opportunity comes up that may be right for that person, I have a list of people that I can refer to. Oftentimes, people approach me after a speech or training session and say, "Hey, I'm looking for a job," or "I'd like to get in this particular field," or "Do you know of anyone that I can connect with?" So I literally write that on their business card—seeking a job or seeking employment—and I note that in my Contacts list. As a result, I've referred hundreds of people to new job opportunities and helped numerous people connect with each other and help each other out.

Colleagues and Partners

I have another list of contacts—colleagues who do similar work as I do, or people who may have new products, new research, or a new book coming out. And then I have another group of people I might just use as general connections that I stay connected with through communications such as general announcements about upcoming events, activities, interesting articles, job postings, or any other information that might be of interest to them. I am constantly updating my status on LinkedIn so that people know what I'm up to. I spend a lot of time on social media looking for people who have similar interests and backgrounds as me and make a connection. It's all about reaching out to people and building relationships and then making them work for you both.

I stay connected with these people in a very informal way. It's an opportunity many of us miss for turning these contacts into contracts. When it comes time for me to look for a new job or research a new opportunity, or if there's a company recruiting me, I can call some of my contacts or go to my Outlook and do a search for someone in that field or someone who's worked at that kind of company, and I can reach out to them. They are more than willing to speak with me, and to help me. You know why: Because I've stayed in contact with them and have helped them.

Leverage Your Contacts

We are now facing a seven percent or higher unemployment rate in America. More than likely, for each unemployed person applying for a job, there are hundreds more applying for the same job. So it's important to be able to pick up the phone or e-mail a contact and reach out to that person and ask about the job, because most jobs come not just by word of mouth but by employee referral. If you have a contact already working at that company who knows you and is willing to make a recommendation or at least refer you to the recruiter, if nothing else, at least it will get your foot in the door and allow you to get an interview or a phone screening, or some information about the company.

Be deliberate; be purposeful; be thoughtful; and be strategic about how you allow people to come into your life; how you allow contacts to be used; how you capitalize on them; and how you seize opportunities to be a blessing or to receive one. My mentor, Les Brown, used to always say to me: "Shirley, you have to live life on purpose and with a purpose. You have to walk, act, and talk like you have a purpose. You have somewhere to go; you have something to accomplish." We can't get caught up in our day-to-day lives, in the things that we're doing, and be so busy that we forget the opportunities that cross our path. Remember, in Chapter 2 I mentioned that it is better to be prepared for an opportunity and never have one, than to have an opportunity and not be prepared, because you may not get that opportunity again. We have to always be prepared.

So, in your day-to-day life, expect that there's going to be someone who crosses your path. Live a life of expectancy and always expect that you're going to run into someone who needs something you have or someone who has something you're going to need so that you are able to get it. This means that you have to be willing to walk, talk, and interact with people; be open to hearing, open to active listening, open to sharing. Often, when we get so caught up in the hustle and bustle of life we actually let life pass us by and we miss so many of these opportunities that come our way—and we don't even know that we missed them. We may be entertaining someone who can help us move to the next level in our lives and not even know that that person is there for that reason.

Three Steps for Successful Networking

George Fraser is one of the foremost authorities on networking, building effective relationships, and leveraging business contacts. George Fraser wrote a great book called *Click: Ten Truths for Building Extraordinary Relationships* (McGraw Hill, 2007) in which he outlines the difference between networking and clicking, and how to overcome the biggest mistakes that people make when they're networking. It's really about creating a win-win situation. He writes that the biggest mistake people make in networking is that they think that's the only step in the process of making contacts with people, while actually there are three. The three steps George Fraser writes about in his book are the same things that I've been doing with my business cards: putting them in my database, following up, and using specific situations to make contact with those contacts, whether it's for a job, a new product, or a great conference they should attend, or whether it's a great article. Let me review the three steps as Mr. Fraser presents them.

1. Identify

The first step he lists for successful networking is the identification phase. This is literally finding people with whom you want to build a relationship. Some of these people, as I mentioned, you meet along the way, at a shopping mall or on the elevator, for example; or you meet them at a conference, or through a mutual friend, or from a colleague at work, or even at church. But when we gather those business cards, that's only the first step; we can't stop there. We have to move to the second step, what Mr. Fraser calls connecting.

2. Connect

We have to proceed from the identification stage to the connecting stage. That's where you cultivate, nurture, and build the relationship. You follow up with the person within a reasonable amount of time. Ninety-nine percent of the people who make contacts and get business cards never follow up. Taking that business card out of your pocket or out of your Rolodex and then e-mailing, calling or making contact with that person is only the beginning of building that relationship— that's a critical stage and most people don't even get there.

3. Click

The third step he describes is called clicking. That's when two or more people connect with each other and they create this common ground; they add value to each other and they create synergy where one and one not only makes two, but it makes eleven. That's the clicking process. He writes that in order to click you have to make sure that these three things are in order. And that's still just the beginning because there are three more things that you need to make sure are in alignment. He writes: "In order to have a true personal relationship and to let it work for you, you have to have chemistry, fit, and timing." In the chemistry stage, there is a kind of energy and karma, an attraction and connection between two people. You're feeling them and they're feeling you. And that attraction may not be physical at all because we're talking in terms of business arrangements too. That attraction might be their attitude. You might be attracted to their passion, their heart, their soul, their spirit, their goals, or even their dreams and their purpose.

The next thing you have to have is fit. Fit is about having that alignment, having compatible goals and objectives, and seeing the world similarly; having some of the same values and aiming in the same direction, and having the same dreams and purpose. Then the third thing you have to have is timing. Timing is what the current situation requires—making sure that the timing is relevant. He writes that all three of these are very important; and it makes me think about how, over time, timing has been critical for me, being at the right place at the right time and meeting the right person. Never underestimate the importance of timing.

5. Strategic Alliances and Partnerships

The above principles segue into the next type of relationship, number five, which is building alliances and strategic partnerships. This is different from networking. You delve more into clicking and making the connections and turning contacts into contracts or job opportunities and promotions and, ultimately, into making more money. It's important to build and find and identify, as Fraser mentions, the relationships that you can then turn into strategic alliances or partnerships. Often, this basically means that you're looking to formalize the relationship—and sometimes it can even be informal—to bring together two entities or more who will work together to achieve something that individually they couldn't do successfully on their own. This is happening with more and more organizations and corporations, which are building more collaborative relationships and partnerships. We're not necessarily always trying to fight the competition; sometimes we have to engage in what I call "coopertition." You have to cooperate and collaborate with each other—including your competitors. Ultimately, you take your core competencies—your skills, your gifts, your strengths—you marry them together, merge them together, and then you have a better organization. In your case as an individual, you can become much more successful when you align yourself with other people who have skill sets that you may not have.

In today's collaborative, customer-driven, networked economy, more and more organizations are building these kinds of relationships with their customers, their suppliers and other partners because of the need to become more competitive, to build a more sustainable business model, and certainly to be more profitable. Organizations like churches are beginning to align themselves more and more with other community organizations and partnerships and projects so that they're able to accomplish more together than they could separately. To create alliances and partnerships means that you identify specific people from your network, from the contacts you've made, from the different business cards you've collected or the phone calls that you've been able to follow-up on, and you nurture the relationships that you've begun to develop. You identify what kinds of skills and competencies and strengths they have that complement what you're already doing.

For example, I align myself with colleagues and organizations that may have a competency or an expertise that I don't have so that I am able to provide greater services when I'm bidding on specific projects or responding to Requests for Proposal (RFP). There are areas in which I'm looking to expand my knowledge, such as technology or social media, because that hasn't been an area of expertise for me, but I partner with other people who have technological expertise and who can provide that service. That helps me to be able to better brand myself on the Internet, to better utilize social media in ways that increase and enhance my brand and my products and services. And it positions me to better market myself to clients, customers, and new opportunities. **RYW**

6. Sponsors

The last type of relationship is that of an advocate or a sponsor, even a champion. This is a critical relationship. I touched on it a bit when

I was addressing mentoring because people often use sponsor and mentor interchangeably; while they're not necessarily the same, there is some overlap. A mentor is somebody who acts as a resource and a role model, someone who offers you advice and counsel and provide perspectives from their experience, and even gives you constructive criticism, whereas a sponsor can be a mentor who does all of those things and more. A sponsor is going to take it to another level by being an advocate on behalf of the person they're mentoring or coaching with respect to advancement and providing other strategic opportunities, such as job promotions. It might be a special new assignment, a new role, or a stretch assignment to help you grow new and different skills and hopefully to even get you greater visibility. A sponsor is someone at a higher level who has enough experience, influence, and credibility in the organization, and who is committed to you becoming a leader or to you accepting a certain role or taking on a greater responsibility in the organization. A sponsor will be able to speak on your behalf when you're not in the room but the decision makers are.

We may think that having a mentor is enough to get us promoted or to get us visibility in an organization to the executives or to the decision makers, but this is often not the case. Sometimes the mentor may not be in a position or have the level of credibility or status in the organization to be able to help you get to that next level or to get the visibility you need. So you need to ask yourself, first, is the mentor I have someone who can help me achieve my career goals or help me move up and around the organization? If the answer is no, the mentor doesn't have sufficient responsibility or doesn't have the tenure or the level of influence to be able to help you get there, then you want to find someone who can, and that may mean a sponsor.

I was reading an article published by the *Harvard Business Review* entitled, "Why Men Still Get More Promotions than Women" (September, 2010).Yes, we are still asking this question and still having this conversation in today's age, especially when women now make up nearly 50 percent of the workforce, and yet we don't see that reflected at the top of our organizations, on boards, or even at the CEO level. The article identifies some challenges of emerging women in the workplace as well as mentoring programs, and it makes the distinction between mentoring and sponsorships as I do here. It also states that men are better at finding career-building mentors than women are.

There are many surveys that indicate that high-performing women tend to be overmentored yet undersponsored relative to their male peers. What this says to me is that we—"we" meaning women, and "we" meaning people of color or minorities—have to do a much better job of building these relationships and cultivating them in a way that creates an effective outcome. Whether it's a new promotion, a different kind of a job, a stretch assignment, a new project, or just greater visibility in the organization, we have to do a much better job of tapping into this very effective tool and identifying sponsors who can help us get the visibility we need, and who can help us grow and give us the great feedback we need, and even challenge us to push beyond our own limits.

Seeking Out Mentors and Sponsors

People ask me: "How do I get a mentor?" "How do I build a relationship that would be meaningful, that results in a win-win relationship?" "How do I get a sponsor, or how can I ensure that my relationships are healthy and wholesome and meaningful, but not toxic?" I tell them: "You need to be selective about the people you surround yourself with." "You want to know what you want out of life, what you want out of your career, what you want out of the company you're working for or the company for which you're looking to start." So it's important, first of all, that you have done that self-reflection and that you have a good sense of what it is you're seeking and what is your ultimate goal.

The next thing you want to do then is to ask other people who might be good mentors or who might be good sponsors. Ask for recommendations; you might ask your immediate boss, or you could ask some of your peers or counterparts. Look into your network and ask others who they've used as good mentors. Look in your organization at some of the great leaders to find out who out of those leaders has a good reputation, and who excels. Leaders have a great way of influencing other people and building great relationships; they're highly regarded by other people. You'll know who they are in your organization because people talk about those who are at the top; you'll get a good sense of who might be good leaders. Your immediate boss or someone like him or her might be able to help facilitate your search.

Sometimes just have to build up enough courage and the willingness to ask that person if they would be willing to spend an hour with you once a month, or if you could take them out to lunch, or if they could give you 30 minutes of their time once a month or every couple of weeks. However that works for you or however it works for them, it's important to take that first step. Put yourself out there and be willing to engage. It has a lot to do with your image, who you are, how you feel about yourself, what you believe about yourself, and what you know your purpose and your vision to be. Find the right person who can help you achieve those specific goals and that vision and that purpose.

Don't be afraid to step out there and take a chance. And don't be afraid of rejection—all they can do is say no, and it's always possible that they'll make some recommendations for you. So don't be afraid to go after what you want. There are particular reasons why we have people in our lives. There are particular seasons that those people will be in our lives, and we have to look for those opportunities and seize every moment we have with the people who cross our path, and leverage those connections into win-win relationships—a win for you and a win for them as well. **RYW**

A final thought on important relationships. Make no mistake about it, while I believe that there are six types of relationships that we'll have with other human beings here on earth, the most important relationship is the vertical spiritual relationship that we have with our God. I believe that none of our horizontal relationships can ever be successful or fulfilling without filling the void of a spiritual relationship with our creator. I believe it's the basis and the foundation for who we are, what we believe, how we behave, and how we engage our other relationships.

My Personal Experience with Toxic Relationships

Let me share a personal story here about toxic people. Some of my greatest lessons in life have come from relationships and particularly from toxic people in my life whom I've had to first identify as toxic, and then confront, and ultimately eliminate. I had to ask myself as I looked in the mirror what I was doing to first attract that person? What energy was I putting out there that brought them into my life? I also had to ask myself why I had allowed them to stay as long as they did and to have the effect on me that they did? Ultimately, I had to ask myself why I needed them. What was it about them or about me in my own life that allowed them to be here?

I've had toxic friends, toxic family members, bad bosses, and toxic coworkers who set out to destroy me, sabotage my career, and mess up my good standing in the organization. Whether they were trying to undermine projects I was working on or just outright stealing my ideas or not giving me proper credit, or whatever it was, these were toxic relationships. I've even had significant others in my life who were toxic, and sometimes these can have the greatest impact, because they are the ones closest to you. But because of my gift and my calling and this passion I have to coach and to train and to empower others to go to the next level in their lives, I've had people come and go in my life whom I've

Remember: The *Reinvent Yourself Workbook* provides exercises, reflection questions, and personal assessments based on the material presented in this chapter. WHEN YOU SEE THIS SYMBOL **RYW**, IT MEANS THAT THERE IS A CORRESPONDING EXERCISE OR ACTIVITY FOR YOU TO COMPLETE. Working these exercises will help you to better integrate the material and focus your efforts towards reinventing yourself and achieving success in moving to the next level in your life. Visit **www.drshirleydavis.com/store**.

coached and trained. And I often found that, as I talked to them about their issues and some of the experiences they had growing up, I could relate to them because I've had some very similar experiences. I grew up as the oldest child, the only daughter with three brothers, and I was very close to them. We were a very close-knit family and I helped my parents. When they were both working, I helped care for my younger siblings. I was responsible for cooking meals, cleaning up after them, making them do their homework, giving them baths, and sometimes disciplining them. I acted like a mom to them. Even today, we're still very close, and they still look to me as big sister and that maternal figure.

That nurturing and loving and protecting mentality followed me into my adulthood. It had a good side, obviously, but there was a not-so-good side that I had to learn the hard way. The not-so-good side is that I allowed people in my life who had what I call the clipped-wing or broken-wing syndrome. They needed someone who would reach out to them, rescue and protect them, nurture them and care for them, and do all the things for them that either their moms did for them or that someone didn't do. Honestly, it made me feel needed and it made me feel significant and important. Don't get it twisted; I learned the hard way that there is a difference between having a personal, healthy relationship and giving outreach to people who are in need or helpless.

At first, for a season, I felt that need. I felt that I was wanted, and I felt important to someone, and I felt safe. It even gave me this false sense of security. At the same time, I was giving out more than I was getting back and I found myself feeling this void in my life and this level of emptiness. I felt used and I felt abused, that someone was taking advantage of my vulnerability and even my own personal experiences.

What I learned through this is that you don't have to immediately open up your heart and invest yourself with every single person who comes into your life. Sometimes you need to take a step back, size up the relationship, and make a determination as to why this person is here, what they need, and how you choose to engage in the relationship. When you know the difference and you behave accordingly—and this is what I began to learn—you don't confuse outreach with love and commitment in a personal and close relationship. I've learned also to be very selective in who I allow in my very closest circle of friends and to whom I open up my heart and my soul. I feel like I'm a very transparent person, but there is a line that you have to draw between how much you're willing to open up and share and trust and give people the benefit of the doubt and how much you give those who you've learned will hurt you or intentionally use and abuse you.

I've always prided myself on being the kind of person who saw the best in other people and assumed the best, positive intent. So when I got into personal relationships and had significant others, I found myself in relationships with persons who were either very needy or who were just using me as a crutch. I had to learn, even in those relationships, that while it was important to me to be in a healthy relationship, I really didn't know that it wasn't healthy for me until something inside of me, my spirit, started to let me know that this relationship was not helping me, that it was hindering me. I was not becoming a better person; as a matter of fact, I was more frustrated and had more anxiety than when I was alone.

I remember being in a relationship with a man who was a master manipulator, a man who was able to identify immediately my weaknesses and vulnerabilities. He listened adeptly and keenly to where I had the greatest needs and was very skillful and artsy in being able to tap into those things. He wined and dined me and gave me wonderful gifts, all the things any woman wants when she's being wooed and pursued by a man. But I found out later that he had a major character flaw and no intention of being in a committed relationship, certainly not in a monogamous relationship where I was the center of the relationship or the most important person in his life. It makes one feel completely insignificant when you find out that the person giving you all these gifts and taking you out and wining and dining you and telling you all these wonderful things and planning this great life with you was telling five or six or ten other women the same thing. It's a very hurtful thing when you feel that level of betrayal, especially when you've been very, very close to a person and you saw the best in them and you felt like you could really trust them.

So we have to open up our eyes and not get so personally involved too quickly; be willing to step back, listen to our closest friends who may be giving you a heads-up that something isn't right about this person, and, most importantly, to what's going on inside you. Your spirit will discern and remind you: "You know, something's just not right about this person." Never underestimate the power of your gut; your spirit knows when something in another person is not right. Don't be so needy and so desperate to be in a relationship with someone else. Don't think because they have all of the external things you are looking for that you can be remiss in looking for the things that count the most—and those are the things that are on the inside, not the outside.

Yes, we're always looking for a man who has a great job or at least a good, steady job, a man who's going to share the same values, a man who respects family and has the spiritual foundation that you're looking for. But those are the kinds of things that take time and for which you have to invest a lot of energy in finding out, not the external things like a great body, great looks, wonderful hair—all those other things that will eventually droop and fall anyway.

That's just a little bit about my story—about how I've had to learn a lot of tough lessons in life because early on I was looking at relationships from a very shallow perspective. Make the right decisions around relationships by utilizing your strengths, your character traits, and your values. **RYW**

Summary

- Assess your relationships. Do you have healthy, happy, nurturing relationships?
- Or do you have toxic people around you—people who are always trying to tear you down, speak negative things, and give off negative energy into your life, people who really don't have your back? And if the latter, why?

- Categorize your five closest friends. How many are a healthy, wholesome influence, and how many are unhealthy or toxic or don't have your back?
- There are five ways to cope with toxic people: confront them, eliminate them, tolerate them, be selfish (take care of yourself), and pray for them.
- There are six types of relationships: Personal relationships, effective mentoring relationships, authoritative relationships, key contacts, alliances or partnerships, and advocates or sponsors.
  - » Personal relationships—those closest to us, family and friends, who have a direct impact on our life, our values, our character, our beliefs, and our habits.
  - » Effective mentors—people who can help you increase your professional effectiveness, your communication skills, your ability to influence and negotiate.
  - » People in authority—anyone who has direct leadership and authority over you, whether it's in the workplace, in a community setting, at church, or in civic activities.
  - » Key contacts—these are relationships that have the potential of providing you with a service or referral, a discount or a product, (on a reciprocal basis), relationships you can leverage.
  - » Alliances or partnerships—these are persons with whom you cooperate and collaborate (sometimes even when you compete) for your mutual benefit.
  - » Advocates and sponsors—these are individuals who are committed to you and take mentoring to a higher level by coaching, providing strategic opportunities, helping you to grow and take on greater responsibilities.
- Don't forget the most important relationship—the one with your Creator. Having a spiritual foundation and something that guides and grounds you and informs your decisions is critical to all of your other relationships. I believe that your vertical relationship with God influences the effectiveness of your horizontal relationships.

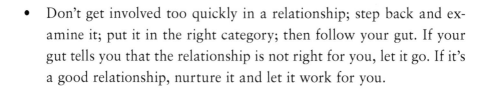

- Don't get involved too quickly in a relationship; step back and examine it; put it in the right category; then follow your gut. If your gut tells you that the relationship is not right for you, let it go. If it's a good relationship, nurture it and let it work for you.

CHAPTER SEVEN:
Repairing Your Finances and Reestablishing a Financial Management Plan

The Financial Shifting

AS A NATION, WE'VE FACED SIGNIFICANT CHANGES over the past few years, many of which have very personal consequences. Some of us have experienced career setbacks or transitions, relationship changes, technological advances—changes happening at the speed of light.

The most daunting change of all is the global economic and financial crisis that has loomed over us for several years and is still volatile today. Millions of Americans have faced home foreclosures; we've seen the value of our homes decrease. Some of us have actually seen our homes go completely under water or upside down, which means that what we owe on our house is far greater than what the house could sell for.

Some of us have even experienced our pay being cut, while others have lost their jobs altogether and now find themselves standing in long unemployment lines. We've seen much of our retirement savings evaporate. Wall Street has crashed and businesses have failed, and many of our dreams have faded under the financial avalanche—this tsunami called "recession." And once again, we find ourselves experiencing another shift. We're at a crossroad of change and we need to reposition and reevaluate, redefine and refocus, and, in the case of our financial situation, we find ourselves having to repair and reestablish a financial management plan. So allow me in this chapter to be open, honest, transparent, and practical, because when our money is funny, it is no laughing matter. Being in a financial crisis affects our peace of mind, our health, our relationships, our will, and our future.

Time to Adopt a New Mindset about Finances

First, I want to address mindset and will. It's not going to help you if I recite a bunch of tips, strategies, and principles if you don't walk away with a different way of thinking and a different will or desire to change your habits, your attitudes, and your approach in the way you deal with your finances. We can only criticize the government, the unethical bank practices of the mortgage companies, and the greed on Wall Street so much for this financial crisis. But if you're really honest with yourself, your financial situation probably could have used some repairing long before the 2008 mortgage crisis hit. And while we all agree that this financial crisis made some bad situations worse, and that it hurt many who were in a good financial position, we can also all agree that there are some lessons we can learn and some things we can do differently in the area of personal finance. As good as I believed I was doing financially, I still found myself negatively impacted, and learning about things I could have done differently.

I bought a house that I could afford at the time, but then I experienced the value of my house decrease by thirty percent. It's now considered under water. I suffered a significant loss of money I had set aside for retirement. Even my company went through budget cuts and pay freezes, and I was left having to shift and do things differently with my finances. We all can learn from these experiences and adopt a new mindset as to how we think about and manage our finances.

My Personal Financial Crisis and What I Learned

I'll be honest too and say that there were some lessons I had to learn years ago in managing my finances. I had to become much more efficient and a much better steward over my money long before this financial crisis hit us. I'm one of those people who believe that you can't teach what you don't know, and you can't lead where you don't go yourself. So allow me to share with you a bit about my own journey. I'll be very transparent and personal so that you can learn from my mistakes and implement some of the strategies I learned that have now put

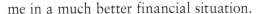

me in a much better financial situation.

A number of years ago I found myself going through a divorce. I was faced with all the challenges of single-parenting, but mostly I was faced with a lot of financial obligations. Many of you can relate to the financial pressure that comes along with parenting in general, let alone with single-parenting. I've been where many of you are right now. Back in those days I would characterize myself as being flat broke, living paycheck to paycheck, not being able to make ends meet—in effect, going through a financial crisis like the one we're recovering from right now.

I'm going to go down the list of things I had to deal with 15 to 20 years ago when I was living in what I would call a poverty situation, and with a poverty mind-set. I had a lot of debt; I wasn't paying my bills on time; I was paying dollar by dollar. I was robbing Peter to pay Paul, as they say, and writing checks that I hoped and prayed would clear the bank in some miraculous way, because I knew that I didn't have the money.

I was borrowing money and getting cash advances from credit cards. I was taking out loans from check-cashing companies—you know the ones I'm talking about; they would take your car title or your jewelry as collateral, and if you didn't pay, then they got themselves a new car or some new jewelry. I was selling personal property at pawn shops just to pay basic bills. I was even getting some high-interest loans—those 25 to 30 percent interest loans—while at the same time, I didn't know how I was going to repay those loans. In the situation I was going through, I needed the money right then; I wasn't planning or even worried about how I was going to pay the loans back years down the road. I was worried about how I was going to be able to take care of my child and myself right then and there.

The Real Price of Borrowing

I didn't sit down and come up with some kind of plan for how I was going to get the money to repay $5,000. I also didn't know that it was probably going to take me 10, 15, 20 years just to pay back $5,000 if all I was paying was $10 to $15 a month at a 25 to 30 percent interest rate. I was using these lending companies like they were banks. I would then go to consumer credit counseling organizations, who would tell me that they would work with some of these credit card companies, lower my credit card rates, and help me to get the payments down and get me out of debt. I was even contemplating bankruptcy at one point. And the list goes on.

I know that a lot of us, given the economy we're in, are facing these same challenges right now, but I also want you to know that there is light at the end of the tunnel—even though that light may appear very far away or very dim when you're in the midst of this kind of financial situation. I lived in that situation for a number of years. I was in bondage; I was stressed out; I was losing weight; I really couldn't concentrate. I was working really hard and yet I didn't feel like I was getting the money I needed to pay the bills because I had a seven-month-old little girl who was completely depending on me. During that period of years, I went through what I call "a process." It was a journey. One day I got tired of being sick and tired. I had been living this way for years—from paycheck to paycheck; I really didn't know how I was going to make ends meet.

Dear God...

I reached a point one day when my daughter was still very small—maybe a year old—and I was standing in my living room in my very small apartment, and I stood before her, I stood before God, and I stood with myself, and I prayed that day: "God, if you get me out of this, I promise I'll never get into it again." I know we have all prayed that prayer, but this time, I meant it. I had prayed that same prayer many times before, but this time I had hit rock bottom and I needed a change.

So I had this conversation with myself, with my God, and with my daughter, and I made all of us a promise that I was going to get out of debt. And then I promised that I would never get back into debt again; that I would never be broke again. I meant it in my heart; I meant it in my spirit; and I meant that I was going to do whatever it took to make the shifts and the changes I needed to make in my life. And I knew it meant that I would have to make some sacrifices, and some difficult choices; and it meant getting some counseling, some coaching, having some accountability; it meant taking control of the way I was living and taking control of my financial situation. It meant that now I had to take a journey. I had to go through a process, with a step-by-step plan. It meant creating a strategy. It meant having the right resources and the right network around me that I could implement in order to make something happen. And, most importantly, it meant adopting a new and different mindset.

I also recognized that it took me years to get into debt; I knew that getting out of debt wasn't going to be an overnight miracle. I wasn't playing the lottery so I knew I wasn't going to hit the jackpot. I wasn't expecting some stranger to walk up to me and give me a million dollars. And I wasn't expecting the credit card companies to automatically wipe the slate clean—although I was praying for some kind of miracle. I began planning and strategizing how I was going to work myself out of that situation I had gotten myself in.

No One Else to Blame

I didn't have anybody else to blame—it was all my fault. I was spending money I didn't have. I had been trying to keep up with certain fads and certain trends and keep pace with the Joneses, so I knew it was going to take me some time because I had gotten into a habit of spending. I had started buying things that were on sale and convincing myself that I was saving money, even though they were things I really didn't need. I had been trying to live a lifestyle I knew I couldn't afford, and I wasn't willing to admit that to myself—until I got to this rock-bottom level. I needed to step down and step back; I needed to take baby steps in order to get to where I wanted to be.

I knew this process was going to take determination and discipline, that it meant denying myself, and that it was going to take perseverance and faith. I knew that I could not revert back to my old habits, but that I was going to have to stick to a plan and a strategy. Finally, I was at a place where I was ready to do that.

Thank you for allowing me to share, to be transparent and open, and even to reveal areas where I've been selfish, greedy, and ignorant about how to manage my money or how to build wealth—and certainly how to save and invest my money wisely.

Now, it's your turn. I am asking you to be as open and honest and transparent as I have been. I am asking you to expose your own areas of weakness, your own areas of selfishness, and to expose areas in which you may be ignorant or lack understanding. This is an opportunity for you to be able to do what I did.

If you have experienced the level of brokenness I just described; if you have hit your rock bottom and are now willing to put in the work and the time that it takes to create the opportunities to make a financial breakthrough, then it's time to develop a new mentality and change the models that got you in financial debt.

The Messages We Heard Growing Up

Think about when you were growing up, and answer these questions:
1. Whether it was taught by words or whether it was modeled by action and deed, what did you learn about money when you were growing up?
2. What did your parents teach you?
3. What was reinforced in your day-to-day life?
4. Whether it was from your parents who raised you or someone else who had influence in your life, what was the message you received about money?

Often when I ask these questions, I get fairly similar responses. A common response is that "My parents (or the people who helped raise me) taught me that money doesn't grow on trees." Or they say: "Money is the root of all evil." Now, of course, we know that's not completely true. It's really the "love of money, or greed, that's the root of all evil."

Other things about money that people say they heard growing up include: "We work hard for the money," or "We can't afford that," or "Money can't buy you love." As we think about some of these things we've heard and that were reinforced from our childhood, into our adolescence and teenage years, and even into our adult years, I guarantee you that these attitudes that have been reinforced in our lives as we were growing up are now shaping our adult habits.

Think about how each of these messages has played out in your adult life. If you were constantly told—and the messages were reinforced—that money is the root of all evil, how has that message informed the way you make decisions and the way you act? If you heard over and over again, "We can't afford that," do you now tend to believe that everything you get is something you can't afford? Do you think you've got to go to the thrift store, or the Salvation Army, or that you've got to borrow money or buy things at garage sales because you can't afford them—even when you really can afford them?

Or have you gone in the opposite direction? Even though you can't afford something, you go into debt by using credit cards, borrowing money, or getting loans to purchase things, because that's what you heard all your life. And now you don't want to hear that anymore; you want to go out and get what you want, regardless of whether you can afford it or not. Think about how each of these messages has played out in your life. It could be unconsciously; it could be subliminally. If you begin to reflect, those messages that have been embedded in your life and followed you into your adulthood now inform your financial attitudes. But it's not too late to change. **RYW**

Principles for Achieving Financial Success

Allow me to share with you some success principles and some life lessons that I've had to learn in my adult life through hard knocks and mistakes. Let me share the process and the journey I walked through to overcome that despair, to eliminate that poverty mindset, and to climb out of the deep recesses of debt, so that today I am financially stable and thriving, and living in what I consider overflow and abundance. Not only am I able to buy what I need, but I can enjoy buying what I want.

I want you to think about why you were created. I want you to understand that you were created with certain gifts, talents, and resources that give you the potential and the ability to be prosperous. There is not one of us who doesn't have certain gifts, talents, and resources that give us the ability and the potential to find our ticket to prosperity—marketable abilities that can produce an income. For example, when you get a job, you have to sell the skills that you can bring to that job; there is some talent, some idea, some expertise, or some gift that you have that allows other people to buy into you—you have something you can sell that is marketable.

Assess Your Gifts and Talents

Let's take a gift inventory—a talent assessment. Take a moment and list the things you are really good at, the things that you believe can produce wealth. What are you gifted at doing? What can you do with your hands better than anybody else? What might there be in your mind that you can share that can make money? Sit down and create a list of all the things you enjoy doing and that you're really good at. Recall some of the things that friends and family members have always told you that you are really talented in—things that you would do and never have to get paid for. Think about things you would enjoy doing if you knew you couldn't fail—things you would do day in and day out. These are the kinds of things you need to think about as you identify your gifts and your talents.

You also want to think about what's in your mind that you can do— what information or skills or techniques you can share that could make money. Knowledge is the new currency. I am making money because of the knowledge I have about human resources, leadership, business strategies, organizational transformation, global workforce trends, and about how to create sustainable business models.

I'm making money on my gifts. I love to speak, and I make money speaking. I'm an international professional speaker. I'm a trainer and a facilitator—I love to create and lead training programs and workshops. I was called to do it; I'm gifted to do it; and it's a gift I knew I had at an early age. And when I realized it, I began to develop my gift, and ultimately I mastered it.

Perfect Your Gift

You have to hone your gift. Over time you have to nurture your gift, master it, and ultimately perfect it, because the greater the development, the greater the marketability, and ultimately the greater the income level. And as you perfect your gift, you must ensure that you keep your self-esteem and your sense of self-worth intact. Yes, you've got to know who you are first of all. Then, you've got to feel good about who you are. And once you know that, you will have no problem mastering that gift and that talent you have inside. But it starts with feeling good about who you are and the value you bring.

The Need for Stable Income

Another principle I learned in the process of coming out of debt is the need for stability. We must have stable bills for stable income, which means bills that are proportionate to that income. This means that no bills should be dependent on money that may not even come in. For instance, if you have a job and you know you're going to receive a stable salary, you can base your bills and set your financial management plan on that income. This is what I call "stable income."

You know that there are going to be some bills you receive every month: such as the utility bill, your car note, or your insurance bill; you know you have to pay regularly for food, for the rent, or for your mortgage. Then there are some things you can't predict—unexpected things that come up, such as car repairs, emergencies, or medical bills. (I will address how to prepare for unexpected expenses a little later in the chapter.)

Stable bills are consistent. We know these bills are coming regularly, and we know that we need to pay these bills based on what money we know is coming in. Basically, we need to plan our lifestyle on what we know we can afford.

Determining Discretionary Money

What does this mean for people who work on commission? Commissions do not necessarily guarantee a stable income, but you can do a couple of things. You may want to make sure that there's a base salary, that you're living off that base salary, and that you set your financial management plan to that base. This way, at least you know what money is promised to come in. Some people receive a base pay and then they receive a commission on top of that. In this case, you want to base your financial management plan on that stable base, and then what comes in on top of that—your commissions—you add in as what I call your "discretionary money."

A second option for determining your discretionary money is to look at your commissions over the last six months of the year (this lets you look at each season). What's been the average? And how do you figure the average? One way is to look at the minimum that you know you're going to have coming in; another is to take 50 to 60 percent of the amount that's come in over the last six months or so and consider that as your average—this is your stable income. You want to make sure that you have stable bills for that stable money and that they are in alignment and in proportion with your income, and not in excess of it.

Increase Your Income or Decrease Your Spending

Do you need to increase your income, or do you need to decrease your spending? It's often the latter—decrease the spending. It's not as easy to increase your income, especially in the kind of economy we've been experiencing over the past five years. The average merit increase now runs between two and two and a half percent, three percent at the most.

One way to increase your income might be to get an extra job or take on a part-time gig. Or, if you're in sales and you have the ability to increase your client base or to go back to certain clients to increase sales, you may be able to increase your income that way. Usually, however, it's easier and more effective for us to look at ways we can cut our spending.

If you cut your spending, or if you increase your income, make sure that you have profit left over. You don't want to live in a cycle of debt and with a poverty mentality. Profit is what you have left over after your transactions have been completed. This means that you have money left over after you spend what you need to spend. It means that after you have paid your bills you have a surplus. So whatever transactions you make, whether it's buying things on sale, making purchases, or paying your bills—whatever it is—it's called a profit if you have something left over. Your goal is to decrease your spending so that at the end of the month, you have that profit.

Zero Balance

Ultimately you want to reach a zero balance in your financial management plan because it's important that you account for every dollar, every penny, and that you decide what you're going to do with your surplus. For example: if you have $50 left over after you've paid all your bills at the end of the month, then that $50 needs to be accounted for. Whether you're going to put it in your savings account, or you're going to pay extra toward a bill, or you're going to make a donation to a charitable organization—whatever you decide to do, you need to account for every dollar, including that extra $50, all the way down to zero. This means that you now have accountability; that you know exactly where all of your money is going. This is called having a zero balance; this is called being accountable for the profit.

Along these same lines, remember that it doesn't matter how much money you make per se. What matters is how much you have left over, or how much you save. A lot of people get caught up in how much money they make. "I make $100,000" or "I make $200,000 or \$300,000." It's no big deal if you're making \$300,000 a year and you're spending \$400,000, or if you're making \$100,000 and you spend \$101,000—you're still creating a deficit. You're still in a cycle of debt. So your target is to make sure that you have profit left over and that you have a zero balance—you are accounting for all the monies, however much you've been able to increase your income or how much you've been able to save your money.

A Rise in Income is Not Permission to Spend

Another practical tip that helped me through the process of coming out of debt was to realize that whenever I got a raise or a new job or even received money unexpectedly, that didn't mean I now needed to increase my spending. Often, when we get a raise or we get unexpected money or even a bonus, the first thing we think about is how to spend it. "Oh, wow, that means now I can get a new car," or "I should go out and buy a new living room set," or "I want a bigger house."

That mindset will put you right back where you started, and then you've enslaved yourself again at a higher price. Instead of increasing your savings you're now increasing your standard of living, and usually increasing your spending, which in turn tends to override what you're actually making, so now you're still living paycheck to paycheck even though you got a new raise.

When you receive extra money or you get a promotion, you do want to adjust your financial management plan or your budget. But you also want to make sure that you maintain your standard of living until you are out of debt and you have reset your budget. Use that extra money now to start paying off some of your other debt; or use that money to start investing and saving for the future. Just be careful that you don't exceed your income.

Misplaced Priorities

Here's another area where I see a lot of people struggle, and it's pretty common. (And I was guilty of it myself when I was going through this process a number of years ago.) I can't tell you the number of clients with whom I have had an opportunity to work and to help build their financial management strategy to get out of the pit of debt and despair who fall into this category. When we get an opportunity to peel back the onion and dig a little deeper, and I ask more and more questions about their financial situation, I find that they have misplaced priorities.

We are all guilty of having misplaced priorities at some point in our lives. I work with so many people who come in driving a BMW, a Jaguar, a Mercedes, or some real nice car, and they're all dressed up—they've got on beautiful designer clothes, designer bags, and nice suits, and they're wearing diamond rings and beautiful jewelry, and they're well-manicured and pedicured, and all of that. But, when I look at their accounts, they usually have less than a hundred dollars or only a few dollars in the bank; they are struggling to pay their mortgage or their rent from month to month. They're still living paycheck to paycheck. They have no savings—they look good and they smell good, and they have all the trimmings and all the trappings of looking successful, but they're struggling financially.

This is backward thinking; this is a poverty mentality. And I know how hard it is to want to live a lifestyle and you're not there yet. But it's a cycle that you'll continue to repeat if you don't stop trying to be something or to live a lifestyle that you really cannot afford right now. And this brings me to another tip, or another trap that I am asking you to avoid, which is that people will often buy their wants and beg their needs. This means that you buy all those things you desire and want and even believe you deserve—whether you need them or not—but then you beg and borrow for your needs—those things you really have to have, such as food, rent, insurance, utilities and transportation.

I often find that people will go out and spend money on great vacations and wonderful weekends away, and nice cars and festivals and concerts, and so many other great amenities, but then they go borrow money to pay their rent, their car payment, their insurance, and other basic necessities. So, again, don't buy your wants and beg your needs. Instead—and this goes back to what I addressed above—you need to establish the right priorities. Realize that there are some things you cannot do right now; there are some things you're going to have to sacrifice and cut back on until you get to that level where you are able to afford them.

Failing to Plan is Planning to Fail

I'm not saying there's anything wrong with treating yourself every now and then to a nice dinner or to a nice outfit that goes on sale, or even to a great deal on a weekend getaway. We all need those times to relax and to rest and to retreat. I'm talking about a lifestyle. I'm saying that you need to make sure you're taking care of priorities first, paying down debts, and getting out of that cycle of financial ruin. You've got to live where you are and according to your means, until you can do better. You've got to create a strategy, set some goals, and put together a plan that will get you from this level to the next level. If you don't have a plan, it means you're planning to fail. To remain the same is the same as moving backwards, because life moves forward. Things change. Life moves ahead, so you can't continue doing the same things or life will pass you by.

We need to stop asking for more when we don't have a plan for getting there. We have to have a plan for our lives, for our family, for our career, as well as for our finances. It may take you two years; it may take you five years; it may necessitate having a seven- or ten-year plan. However long it takes, work the plan and stick to it. Be determined and persevere, and you'll be able to accomplish what you set out to do. Go first from point A to point B; ultimately you'll get to point Z—which is to be financially fit, thriving, successful, and free. **RYW**

Change Your Mindset, Change Your Life
When I got mired in debt, it took me nearly seven years of being disciplined and cutting back my expenses, of being really cognizant of my spending and making different choices—and denying myself. I had

to make sacrifices and ultimately change my habits and my mindset. I even had to question myself sometimes as to the motive, the "why"— why was I buying something or why did I want something. And oftentimes it came back to something quite shallow or something selfish. So you have to check yourself and shift your mindset, and understand the reasons and the intentions why you even buy certain things that right now you know you can't afford. During those seven years of digging myself out of that pit of debt, I learned how to not get back into debt; it became a lifestyle change for me. The choices I made became part of my psyche, my thinking.

As you set your plans in place, and as you create goals, it may involve doing things as simple as cutting back on how often you do something, such as going to the hairdresser less often. Perhaps you only go once a month instead of every single week. It may be that you purchase your own hair care products and do your own hair. Your plan may mean changing to a simpler hairstyle or maybe not getting your nails done in acrylics and just using some clear fingernail polish for a while. It could mean going to the grocery store with a list and sticking to your list. Or you might take along an accountability partner to make sure that when you go shopping you only get what you need and what's important, instead of what you desire and things on sale that you really don't need. Your strategy could be to purchase a used car rather than a brand-new car with all the bells and whistles that you really don't need. It could be something as simple as cutting back on your cell phone bill by downgrading some of your options and features. There are so many

Remember: The *Reinvent Yourself Workbook* provides exercises, reflection questions, and personal assessments based on the material presented in this chapter. WHEN YOU SEE THIS SYMBOL **RYW**, IT MEANS THAT THERE IS A CORRESPONDING EXERCISE OR ACTIVITY FOR YOU TO COMPLETE. Working these exercises will help you to better integrate the material and focus your efforts towards reinventing yourself and achieving success in moving to the next level in your life. Visit **www.drshirleydavis.com/store**.

different tips and tools you can incorporate for getting yourself out of debt, and for shifting and changing your mindset. By doing some of these simple lifestyle changes, it can change your financial situation.

I'm trying to make my tips for getting out of debt very simple and very practical, but remember: You don't have to be rich to be profitable, but to be profitable you do have to be practical. We all have something we can bring to the table, something we can use—and we are all at different stages and different levels and at different places in our lives. So, in the most practical sense, we all have to do what makes sense for us and what works best for us. We can't get caught up looking at somebody else and trying to do what other people do. What works is going to vary from person to person, so as I present these tips and these principles and these strategies, you have to make sure that you are applying them in a practical way; you have to make sure that you're thinking about them in your context and according to your ability and your willingness, and your level of commitment, and your level of faith. **RYW**

Saving Money for the Future

Now I want to address an area that is critical as you are repairing your finances and re-establishing your financial management plan. It's a principle called "Saving Money for the Future." And that future could include unexpected expenses, such as when your car breaks down or you get a flat tire, or when your refrigerator goes on the blink or your washer and dryer go out and you have to get new ones. What if your power goes out for five days and you lose your food? (That happened to me last summer.)

You also want to save money for family emergencies or illnesses that you can't anticipate. And you certainly want to be saving money for your future plans—things you have in store for moving to the next level. It could be your children's college fund, retirement, starting a business, or buying a new house, or even your retirement home. You've got to be able to save. I know some people adopt the mentality, "If I've got the money, I'm going to spend the money. I'm going to enjoy it while I've got

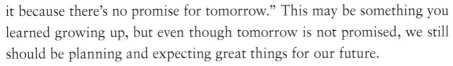

it because there's no promise for tomorrow." This may be something you learned growing up, but even though tomorrow is not promised, we still should be planning and expecting great things for our future.

You also may need to be planning for when you have no more tomorrows, such as estate planning, drawing up a will or setting up a trust, purchasing life insurance, and planning for your funeral. That's all part of saving money for the future and taking care of things for when your tomorrows are limited.

Consider the Unforeseen

We know that we are going to experience trials and tests and unexpected circumstances that are outside our control. But we've got to be sure that we're still planning even though we can't always predict what's going to happen next. This is the thing we call "life." Right? Life happens. And you don't want to live in such a frivolous way that you can't respond—you don't want to lose everything simply because you didn't save for a rainy stormy day—or a hurricane, a sickness, a fire, or anything else.

Make sure that you're putting money aside so that you can be in the position to respond to these unfortunate situations. Think about renter's insurance, homeowner's insurance, car insurance. Consider home warranties such as American Home Shield or HMS, so that by paying a small deductible you can call your warranty company when appliances break down in your house, and they take care of the replacement or repair costs. There are a number of ways you can prepare for the future, put your money to great use, and protect your property and your possessions.

As a rule, it is recommended that you set aside at least 10 percent of your income. Set aside 10 percent in your savings account that you can liquidate in the event that you may need it. So, if you're making $1000 a month, you need to put aside $100 in a savings account. Another general rule for me personally—and I think other people do this as well—is that

I set aside 10 percent for charitable contributions, such as tithes, offerings to your local church, or donations to your charity of choice.

But please use sound judgment. You may be in a situation where you just can't do the 10 percent. I was in that position too, and so I started out with three percent; then I moved up to five percent; then I graduated to seven percent; and then I progressed up to 10 percent; and now I'm giving more. Determine what percent works for you. You've got to be practical and use some wisdom. Start with what makes sense for you. Start with an awareness of where you are now and where you're trying to get to. The important thing is that you're doing something, that you're setting something aside, and you're getting yourself into the habit and routine of setting aside a savings, so that it becomes a part of your lifestyle—that's an important principle.

Don't Get Caught up Worrying About What Others Think

Another principle is to stop caring what other people think. You've got to get out of that mindset of needing other people's approval, needing other people to validate who you are and what you're doing. People often buy fancy cars and expensive clothes, and all kinds of designer jewelry and stuff like that, just so that other people will think they're rich. Actually, they're merely putting on a façade and trying to keep up the appearance that they're very successful when in fact they're living paycheck to paycheck.

Rich people don't care what you think; rich people aren't necessarily living to make money. Rich people let the money work for them. There's a difference. Some of us work for money; rich folk let money work for them. So we want to make sure too that we're not caught up with what other people think about us. What's most important ultimately is that we are able to say that we're spending the money we have, that we're not exceeding our income and spending beyond what we're able to afford, and that we are building a wealth-management plan so that we have something to look forward to, as well as something to look back on.

Think Beyond Your Day Job

A strategy I've employed over the last 15 years or so has been to develop my skills, my gifts, and my talents to produce income for me above and beyond my day job. With my day job I have a stable paycheck; I receive money every two weeks. The money I earn over and above that I've designated to go into a separate savings account. This is money that I don't touch; this is money that I don't plan to use (unless absolutely necessary)—yet I've accounted for it.

I would encourage you to think about doing the same thing because by doing so you adjust your lifestyle to use only the money in your regular checking account, not the money in your savings account. You should plan not to use the money in your savings account for your daily or monthly bills. That's money that you want to accrue over time so that if you need to pull it out for any reason—any reason that you're going to plan for and account for—then that money is there.

I have a checking account that I use for my stable bills—my utilities, my rent, my insurances, my car payment, my mortgage, and so on—and then I have a savings account where I put money aside for emergencies—or for my daughter's college tuition, or for illnesses, or for anything else I may not anticipate.

Save Money, But Start Small

You can have money taken out of your paycheck every couple of weeks as well; and you don't necessarily miss the money once you start to adjust your lifestyle. You can start out by having $10 deducted from your paycheck every two weeks and save $20 a month, or you can start out by taking more out every two weeks if you can afford to let it go. Let's say, for example, that you've decided not to go to the hair salon every two weeks or every week; now you're only going to go once a month; or maybe you're going to stop going altogether and take care of your own hair. That money that you would have normally used to pay the hair salon you can now allocate to go into your savings account. By decreasing your spending, you can now increase your savings.

Additionally, you want to start putting your money to work. Invest in areas that will allow your money to appreciate rather than depreciate. Money that appreciates is money that pays you a dividend or earns interest as a result of being invested or put into some kind of savings account. For example, if you put money into a CD (certificate of deposit), there is going to be a yield, or an interest rate that you will be paid, as a result of the bank having your money. You are more likely to receive more from a CD than from a savings account, but even savings accounts have some small percentage of yield, so you can expect to get at least some money back. Even if it's one percent or only one quarter of a percent, that's still more money than you had before. And the more you continue to save, the more it's going to accumulate over time. This is called appreciation; this is making your money work for you.

When you purchase a house, you expect that over time the market is going to reset itself and that at the end of a period of time that house will increase in value, and you'll be able to sell that house for more money than you put into it. This is also an example of appreciation.

We are constantly spending our money on things that do not appreciate, such as entertainment, beauty supplies, going to the movies, or buying a car. Cars no longer appreciate in value. Back in the day, we could write off car loan interest on our taxes. Now, not only can you not write off your car; they don't appreciate; they actually depreciate. When we purchase new furniture, or we buy a new flat screen TV or a new entertainment system, none of that is appreciable. These all depreciate over time.

Credit Card Debt

The next thing we have to address in our financial management plan is credit cards. A lot of the issues I had to deal with in getting out of debt came from the credit card debt I had accumulated. That was the biggest amount of debt I was carrying. I had six or seven different credit cards starting from when I was in college; I had credit cards that charged different interest rates—many of them as much as 17, 18, or 19 percent.

I paid just the minimum payment on most of them, and that was definitely the trap, because every time I got another credit card I was given another line of credit. I learned the hard way that by paying just the minimum payment of $10, $15 and $20 it was going to take me years and years and years to pay off that credit card debt.

So as I worked through this process of repairing my credit, one of the first things I did was to cut up all my credit cards; I just stopped buying on credit. The next thing I did was to reach out to consumer credit counseling agencies; I started reading books; and I took a few classes on budgeting and finances and how to get started. I even went to some of the counselors in my church and got some help.

The main thing is that I reached out. I realized that I had to start living on cash. I wasn't disciplined enough and couldn't be trusted with credit cards, so I got rid of the temptation. That was definitely a sacrifice and an enormous lifestyle change, because now I really did have to deny myself. I couldn't go and get any more credit cards because my credit was already really bad. Now I had to make different choices, and I had to live on what I could actually afford—Isn't that a noble idea? But it taught me how to be disciplined and how to make the right choices. So I started to live off cash. I got debit cards for my checking account, and that's how I started to budget. That's how I started to live. Debit cards are like plastic checks; if you don't have the money in the bank, they will be declined. You won't be able to make your purchase.

Paying Off a Credit Card is Liberating

Once I paid off one credit card, then I'd pay off another; I would take that extra money from the first credit card and I'd double up on paying off the next credit card, and then the next credit card. It allowed me to be in so much control; and it helped inform my choices and my decisions. When I would see things that I wanted and think, "Wow! How great would it be to have that!" I could look back at my plan and say, "No. I'm $30,000 in debt, so right now my priority is to make sure that

I am setting myself up for success and financial freedom in my future, and not walking back into that same trap of having a poverty mindset."

It can happen overnight. You can backtrack and literally find yourself back in debt again. So once I paid off my credit cards, I started paying toward other bills—either my student loan, or those unsecured loans that I had gotten, or those check-cashing companies that had given me loans. And then I could start putting money aside that would build up over time and allow me to have the money in my bank account that I could use to be my own kind of lending agency and pay myself back when I needed it. The good news is that now I wasn't being charged any high interest rates by borrowing from myself.

There are times when we are still going to need to use credit. Most of us are not going to walk into a mortgage company and pay cash to buy a house. We are going to have to finance that house. Most of us are not going to walk onto a car lot and buy a new car with $15, $20, or $30 thousand in cash.

I knew that I had to build my credit back up again, and that credit is all about credibility. How much can someone trust you and depend on you to be reliable and committed to your word to pay back the money you were loaned? It took me another six or seven years to get through all the credit card issues, the student loan issues, the delinquencies, and the slow pays. It all impacted my credit, and it took me a long time to get myself out of that situation and to rebuild my credit. Today, my credit is pristine. I've done a really good job of making sure that now I'm protecting my credit, my good name, and my reputation. I can now walk into a mortgage company and get the best rate and negotiate the best fees. I can walk into a car dealership and I can negotiate the best interest rate for financing a car, or I can call my credit union and get instant approval for a loan. This is what having good credit allows you to do. A great credit score will also impact your ability to get a job. A lot of companies will do a credit check just to see if you are credible. They want to know if you are a person of your word; if you have a high level of integrity; and if you are going to be as committed as you say you are.

Be Careful About Lending Money to Family and Friends

Think twice before lending money to close family and friends when you are in debt yourself. You will have to muster up the courage to say "no." I realize this may sound harsh, but it's very important, especially if you are experiencing the kind of financial devastation that I've been talking about. If you are struggling to pay your bills and you're still living paycheck to paycheck, and if you are having to borrow money yourself, how in the world can you afford to give someone else money that you do not have?

Not only is it going to derail and sabotage your efforts to get out of debt, but it has larger implications—the main one being that people probably won't pay you back, and if you expect them to, it can impact your relationship. I encourage you, please stop giving people money you don't have—money you know they probably won't pay back. One of the rules I live by is that I try not to lend money. But if people come to me with a situation and they need to borrow money, I will only give out money that I don't expect to get back. And then I just give it as a gift, without any expectation of getting it back.

The other thing to avoid when you're trying to get out of debt is cosigning loans for other people. You're still trying to work out your own financial management plan and these kinds of decisions can derail your efforts to get there. **RYW**

Take Advantage of Financial Opportunities on the Job

401(k) Matching Plan

Another opportunity that you want to take advantage of as you're repairing your finances and rebuilding your financial management plan is to utilize some of the vehicles that your employer provides, such as a 401(k) matching plan. This is something that you will greatly benefit from later in life. Again, it's all about saving, about looking toward your future—and who wouldn't want to take advantage of money that's being matched? For every dollar you put in a 401(k) plan, your employer may match it up to three and sometimes six percent of your salary. So take advantage of that. I know that often means you've got to decrease the amount of money you can plan for your budget each pay period because that's money you won't see. For example: if you're getting paid $1,000 a month, you may have all of your money budgeted with nothing left over. But you may want think about, if nothing else, putting $20 or $25 in your 401(k) because your employer will match every dollar you put into it, and that's an appreciable gain.

Healthcare Flex Plans

You also may want to take advantage of the healthcare and the flexible spending accounts. If you have children, or medical bills, or prescriptions to be filled, you can set aside a bit of money through your employer into a tax-free flex account from which you're then able to pay for deductibles, copays, out-of-pocket medical expenses, and your medical bills.

Tuition Reimbursement Programs

Tuition reimbursement programs are another great opportunity. That is how I was able to get my master's degree and my Ph.D. I worked at organizations that had a very generous tuition reimbursement program—and many companies do. Many companies have a tuition reimbursement policy that stipulates if you go back to school to gain additional skills and knowledge within the scope of your job, or to develop skills that would be valuable to the organization, they will pay for part or all of the degree program. Some companies pay for education by the class; some will pay a percentage of the cost; either way, it is certainly worthwhile to take advantage of company assistance if you want to be able to increase your value in the organization, your self-worth, and your marketability.

Life Insurance and Training

There are two other things provided by your employer that you can take advantage of, and the first of these is life insurance. Companies will often pay life insurance in the amount of one to two times your salary. And, if you like, you can get even more insurance by paying a small premium. The second thing to take advantage of is any special onsite training your employer may provide. Sometimes employers have partnerships or alliances with different universities so that you can take classes for a subsidized amount. These are two ways you can cut back on your expenses by capitalizing on benefits provided by your employer.

Get Your Credit Report and Know Your FICO Score

Let me share a few more tips that I learned about reestablishing my credit, things that were eye-opening to me and actually helped change both the way I view my credit and the way people made decisions about me. First, make sure that you get your credit report. By law, you are entitled every year to your annual credit report, and it's supposed to be free. You can get it by going to annualcreditreport.com. There are three different credit reporting agencies that track your spending habits, your accounts, and your financial worthiness. These are Equifax, TransUnion, and Experian. You want to review your credit report and make sure it's accurate, because research shows that one in three credit reports contains mistakes. Review your credit report and correct any such mistakes by contacting the credit bureaus that display any errors.

You also want to know your FICO score. Most people don't understand what that is. FICO stands for Fair Isaac Corporation, named after Bill Fair and Earl Isaac who founded the corporation in 1956. Basically, your FICO score will rank somewhere between 300 to 900; the higher your credit score, the more creditworthy and reliable and trustworthy you are—and the better you'll be able to get access to good rates. Your credit report is used for a number of different things. When you apply for an apartment or to get a lease, you will be subjected to a credit report. Mortgage companies and car dealerships pull your credit report; whenever you apply for homeowner's insurance, they will pull your credit report. Cell phone companies and credit card companies will pull it. Utility companies, gas and electric, usually pull your credit report to determine whether or not they're going to charge you a deposit. And now, more and more employers are pulling your credit report to identify whether or not you are creditworthy.

So you need to know what impacts your credit score. Paying your bills on time affects your credit score in a very positive way, but if you make too many late payments, or are delinquent in making payments, or if there are too many hard inquiries from potential creditors on your report, these will certainly be red flags to the credit agencies, and to any company that pulls your credit.

You want to avoid having too many open accounts with large balances at the same time. This is one of the traps that a lot of us get into. Stores such as Macy's, Nordstrom's, Home Depot, Best Buy, and the like, all have credit cards; and they offer 10, 15, or 20 percent off your purchase if you open up a credit card. We apply for the card because we want to get that savings on the merchandise; and then we say to ourselves, "Oh, I'll just pay it off at the end of the month." Just remember, if you continue to have open accounts like this, it's going to have a negative impact on your credit score.

You might ask: "Well, how long does it take to rebuild credit?" The answer depends on how damaged your credit is and how severe any delinquencies have been. For example, if you file for bankruptcy it stays on your account for seven years, and sometimes ten. If you've had write-offs or delinquencies, they will stay on your credit report from three to five years. And then, any lien or judgment placed against you will stay on your account for seven to ten years. It takes a long time to build up your credit, so I can't stress enough the importance of making sure you shift your lifestyle, your habits, and your mindset so that you avoid this kind of setback in the future.

I've covered quite a bit in this segment, but I want to leave you with a few more tips and practical principles on how you can start repairing your finances and reestablishing your financial management plan. I

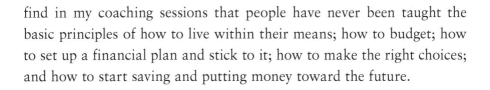

find in my coaching sessions that people have never been taught the basic principles of how to live within their means; how to budget; how to set up a financial plan and stick to it; how to make the right choices; and how to start saving and putting money toward the future.

My Top Ten Tips for Gaining Financial Stability

Tip #1: Determine Your Current Financial State

You need to know your current financial state. You need to know the reality of where your finances are. Most people know that they're living from paycheck to paycheck, but that's not a financial management plan. So the first thing you've got to do is to sit down and establish that financial plan. You need to know exactly how much you are bringing into your household per month, and how much is going out the door.

Tip #2: Contact Your Creditors

This is very hard for many of us because we've become so accustomed to avoiding our creditors. If we've lost our job or we're unable to pay on time or even pay at all, we need to stop skirting around the idea of having that conversation with the person trying to track us down. Confront the situation and take responsibility. Contact them and let them know what your situation is and see if you can work out some kind of arrangement or payment plan or even some kind of deferral.

Your creditors may be willing to work with you, but it is going to cost you a whole lot more if you avoid them, because they are simply going to send you to a collection agency. This in turn is going to tack on attorney fees as well as past-due fees and penalties. So it will benefit you to take the initiative and be proactive in contacting your creditors early on. But notice what I didn't say: I didn't say that you need to secure a third party to make those phone calls for you, to get in touch with your creditors and start the negotiation process. I went through that process fifteen years ago, but I have found out over the years that I really didn't need to pay extra fees for companies to make a phone call I could make myself. They promised they would be able to get my debt eliminated; they promised they'd be able to straighten out my credit and get me back to perfect credit. Some of them even promised they'd be able to negotiate my rates down—and in some cases, that happened. But I also found out that they didn't do anything different or say anything magical that I couldn't have done or said myself. Call your creditors with a simple message like this: "ABC Company, my name is so-and-so, and I'm calling because I'm having some real financial issues right now. I'm not in a position to be able to pay you on time. I'm not even in a position to pay the minimum payment, but I want to work out some kind of arrangement. I have every intention of paying. I know this is my commitment. But out of my own integrity I want to make sure that I am being upfront with you and let you know that I'm not able to pay right now. So I want to find out what payment arrangements we can make based on my current situation."

This simple statement is the same as what I heard the consumer credit counseling companies say. They weren't threatening anyone; they didn't have any magical tactics they were able to use. So call with complete honesty and openness, and be willing to confront the situation and apologize; acknowledge that you are not in any position right now to pay, but that you want to do what's right and manageable for you.

Your Creditors Will Work with You

In most cases, those organizations will be willing to work with you, because at the end of the day they just want you to pay off your debt. They want you to at least make some attempt to pay them back. I encourage you to think about how you can take control and how you can empower yourself to address your situation without having to pay somebody else to do it, just because you feel uncomfortable or you're a little bit afraid. Beware of those organizations or those people who promise you that they can get you completely out of debt, and that they can get you back to perfect credit. That is absolutely untrue; they are trying to take your money. I have fallen victim to that in the past; so trust me, it's a process you have to work out yourself. The three credit agencies are not going to be bought off; and it's simply not going to be that easy for you to be able to demonstrate over a short period of time that you are now creditworthy.

Yes, there are steps you can take, but your credit score is not going to change so significantly that it takes you from a 350 credit score one month up to a 450 score the next, and then a 650 the month after that. That is absolutely not the way the system works. So if anyone promises you something like that, they're just trying to take your money—run in the opposite direction.

You want to be very cautious of those third-party agencies because they are going to charge you fees to do something you can do yourself. And that is money you want to use to pay down your debt. I paid these agencies $30 to $40 a month because they said they could negotiate rates for me and get my credit back perfect. I went through their counseling process on a monthly basis, but, quite frankly, they didn't do anything different than what I could have done myself. I could have saved myself that extra $40 and used it to pay down another credit card. So beware.

Not too long ago I was counseling a client of mine, helping her work toward her financial goals, and trying to help her walk through the whole process of getting out of debt and overcoming her despair. She said very honestly and openly: "I just want to let you know that things are really bad." And I responded: "Okay, I understand that. I'm not here to judge you. I simply want to hear how we can help get you on the right track."

Together we called that first creditor, and we basically said the same thing I presented above: "Hi. My name is so-and-so. I'm having some real financial struggles right now. I've been laid off from my job, and I'm not in a position to pay on time. I really can't even afford to pay the minimum payment right now, and I wonder if there is some payment arrangement we can negotiate that will allow me to still be able to remain in good credit, and also be able to manage based on my current situation."

She was on the phone and she was really shocked that we were able to work out an arrangement right then and there on that conference call. They decided that they would hold off charging her interest rates over the next couple of months; that they would forbear taking any legal action, and in effect enter into a deferral arrangement. She was able to find out on that call how much power she really had by simply owning up to her situation. She talked about how liberating it was just to be able to say, just to be able to acknowledge, "I can't pay right now. But I know I own my responsibility. What can you do to help me in my situation?"

Always Know the Interest Rate

One of the other telling things that came out of my conversation with this client was that she didn't even know how high her interest rate was—it was 25 percent. I find that many people don't even look at how high the interest rate is; they just look at the minimum payment; how much it's going to cost them per month. Again, that's bad financial management. You get a credit card with a 25 percent interest rate, and you may have a $1,500 or a $5,000 credit line. You spend that money and run up your balance—with that 25 percent interest rate—while all you pay per month is $15, $20, or $25. At that rate it will take you 15 years or more to pay off that credit card—provided that you don't buy anything else on it.

So think about that the next time you buy something. You want to know what the interest rate is on your credit card. Then you want to count the costs. If you're going to buy a pair of shoes or a hat or a coat, or whatever you buy, and you're only paying $20 a month on a credit card that charges a 25 percent rate, you've got to figure out how much you are ultimately going to pay for that item. Is it really worth it? For example, if you buy a coat that costs $200 and you're only paying $15 a month at 25 percent interest, and you're paying that over time, you end up paying hundreds more for the coat.

You have to think in terms of how much an item is going to cost over the lifetime of the debt, and this means looking at what the interest rate does to the ultimate cost. This is part of the financial management planning you've got to do. Too often we will not look at the fine print, and we will sign ourselves away, not knowing that we're paying a whole lot more than what the product is worth.

Take Advantage of Free Counseling

Even though I don't recommend that you go to these third-party agencies that promise they can wipe your credit clean, I am not saying that you shouldn't get help from a counselor or a financial coach. There are a number of free agencies or community organizations that will provide you some counseling and coaching free of charge. These are the sources of help I would suggest you find. Look them up in your local community phone book or online; there are even free resources that you can read online. There are books that will walk you through the process of how to build a basic financial plan or a basic budget. You can even contact someone at your church. Many churches now have financial seminars and workshops; I am a financial coach in my church, and we don't charge people to come to our counseling sessions.

So there are many options available for you to get help; someone who's going to hold you accountable; someone who's going to help raise your level of awareness and walk you through this process. It's great to have someone hold your hand while you learn your way through the process—someone who's going to keep you on track and accountable to your commitment. **RYW**

Tip #3: Obtain a Copy of Your Credit Report

You've had a chance to establish where you are financially; you've looked at your current state and assessed your expenses and your income; and you have confronted your reality—that was step number one. Next, you contacted your creditors—that was step number two. Now, it's time to get a copy of your credit report and review it for accuracies and inconsistencies. I hate to say it but most credit identity thefts come from family and friends, sometimes your closest friends. Research shows that most people have their identity stolen by someone who knows their social security number, their address, their previous residences—just enough information to open up new accounts in their name. So review your credit report to ensure that there's nothing on it that you didn't authorize or that you didn't do yourself; and make sure that all of the personal information is correct.

Get a copy of your credit report on an annual basis, at a minimum. Or, if you would prefer, you can also sign up for credit monitoring services on a monthly basis for about $6.95 a month. These companies monitor the activity on your credit report on a daily basis, looking for any instances where there is an inquiry on your account, or a new account is opened, or any time an account is closed—anything that causes your credit score to change. They will send you an alert. They will help you identify anything that looks suspicious and that could ultimately end up being identity theft. **RYW**

Tip #4: Prioritize What Bills You Pay Down First

There are a number of options you can pursue when thinking about which bills to pay down first. Some people decide to pay off their high-interest credit cards or their high-interest loans first. Some people want to go after the high balances first. And there's a third strategy by which some people go after the small bills first, because they want that sense of accomplishment; they want to see a short-term result, a quick milestone, and to build their momentum. People like to pat themselves on the back and feel good about themselves while going through this process. Because we know it's difficult, and it's going to take a long time, going after the small bills first can be very encouraging and motivating.

When you pay that bill off, you can now use the money you no longer have to pay toward that bill and pay down another bill. The last thing you want to do is to look over your credit report after six months or a year and see that you've still got the same number of creditors, and they haven't changed; there's been no movement. But when you are able to knock out at least some of those smaller bills, then you can start knocking out the other ones.

Of course, this all depends on your situation. Every person is different. Every situation is different. So I can't give you a very specific plan for how to approach it—I'm providing general guidance. This is where I definitely recommend that you find a financial coach or someone who knows about financial management planning. You can look in your phone book; you can pull from your community resources; or perhaps you can contact your church for referrals, as I mentioned above. This is the time to have a coach—someone who will cheer you on, hold you accountable, and provide their expertise and knowledge to help you prioritize based on your situation. As I said above, some people make their payments based on interest rate, some on their highest balance, and some on how old the debt is. The fourth area you want to consider is what payment arrangements you've made with your creditors. If you told one creditor that you're going to be able to pay this off in the next 60 days because they agreed not to charge you any interest, or because they excused some of the debt, then you want to go after that debt first. So that's how you prioritize. What's critical and important is that you create a plan, you stick with that plan, and you make sure that you have someone who can help hold you accountable. **RYW**

Tip #5: Set SMART Goals

I addressed this at length in Chapter 3. Remember, SMART is an acronym for Specific, Measurable, Achievable, Realistic, and Time-bound. You can set SMART goals for increments of 30 days, 60 days, six months, one year, two years, or more. For every goal you set, however, it's important that you outline the actions or the tactics you're going to take in order to achieve that goal. And you also want to lay out specific milestones. For example: a smart goal might be that in the next 30 days you're going to contact five creditors to set up financial arrangements on your bills. That's smart and it's specific—you've said specifically that you're going to call those five creditors over the next 30 days; and you included the reason—you're going to set up financial arrangements. It's measurable because you can measure whether or not you call these people. Is it achievable and realistic? Check that yourself. I think so. You have a telephone, and you make the time, and you set down specific guidelines for what you're going to say, your script—more specifically, what you want to get out of that call. And it's time-bound—within 30 days. That's a smart goal.

Another example might be that you set milestones. For example, your first milestone might be that you're going to call your first creditor within week one, and two more creditors by the end of week two, so that by the end of the fourth week (those 30 days) you have laid out a specific schedule for contacting those five creditors. Or you might set a goal that by the end of the year, you're going to pay off two creditors. That's also specific: two creditors by the end of the year. You might want to make the goal more specific by identifying which creditors those are, and whether it's going to be the ones with the highest balance, the ones with the highest interest, the ones that are the oldest, or whatever you decide based on the arrangements you've made with your creditors.

So that's a realistic goal. You can measure it because you said you want two of your creditors paid off. You have set the timeframe for the end of the year. Now you want to also set milestones or checkpoints, whether on a monthly or weekly basis—again, whatever works best for you! You will be the only one to know whether or not you'll need more accountability, or tighter timelines to check in, or if you can trust yourself every month to make sure that you're checking in and paying off those credit cards.

Tip #6: Make it a Family Affair

Get your spouse/partner/significant other involved, and make this a teachable moment for your children. I know this could be a tough conversation because money is a very sensitive topic and can be controversial in a relationship and in a family—but you've got to make the commitment to have the conversation. Let your family be part of the solution. Share with your children how they can contribute, and share with them where they may have been a contributor to some of the financial issues you're dealing with.

Look at this as an opportunity for the family to be accountable for taking specific steps to help decrease the household debt. They can come up with some simple actions they can take to help be a part of the solution: things like turning off the lights when they leave a room or turning off their computers when they're finished because computers use a lot of power. They can also think about making their lunch several times a week rather than taking lunch money every single day, or not having that music or that sound system playing all night long in their ears, or perhaps not pressuring you for all the latest gadgets, such as the latest iPhone or that hot new style of jeans. Perhaps their part is to not make you feel guilty or to not nag you about buying all the latest technology.

My daughter's been asking for the iPhone 5 for a few months, and I've said to her, "Your contract for your cell phone plan is not up until next August, and so I am not going to pay the penalty or the fees associated with upgrading ahead of time." Sometimes they just have to make some sacrifices and be accountable by being a part of the solution and not creating more and more debt. It's a great idea if you would even allow your children to come up with a specific budget as well. For example, if you give them a weekly or monthly allowance, allow them to come up with a real simple budget for what they're going to do with their money, even what they're going to do to save, whether you're giving them $50 a week or $20 a week or whatever amount— teach them about zero balance budgeting. Have them take their $20 and account for every penny; and let them determine how they are then going to spend that money. It's important for us, as parents, to start reinforcing those messages around how to manage money early on. Look at this as an opportunity to teach them about money at an earlier age than most of us received it.

Toward the beginning of this chapter, I asked what you learned from your parents, what messages were reinforced to you about money. We've got to make sure that we're reinforcing positive messages and that we're teaching our children great financial management habits early on, so that we can help them avoid falling off the same fiscal cliffs.

Tip #7: Review Your Goals Regularly

Review your goals monthly, quarterly, and annually. Make sure that you're reviewing your progress with your financial coach or your financial mentor or whoever your accountability partner is—this could be your spouse, your partner, or even your children. Have those family meetings; I encourage those at least once a month.

I recommend that you make a formal review of your goals using someone who has the knowledge and the expertise and someone who's going to hold you accountable. Review where you are; make sure that you make the necessary adjustments and modifications; check in and ensure that you're still on track to achieve those year-end goals you set, and that you haven't fallen off the wagon and reverted to old behaviors.

These reviews are opportunities to think about what specific things you want to do differently. And this is where you want to have your family be a part of that conversation—your spouse or your children or anyone else in the household who affects this financial plan. This is the time for all of you to evaluate what you can continue doing that is working, stop doing what's not working well, or perhaps start doing some new and better things that are going to help you achieve that financial goal.

Tip #8: Journal Your Journey

I can't tell you how therapeutic it was for me to document my journey when I went through this process. I journaled everything I was going through. I wrote down the lessons I was learning, the actions I was taking, the sacrifices I was making, and even the results and the impact

I was seeing in my life—and I was doing this on a weekly, daily, and monthly basis.

I experienced how journaling changed my mindset and the way I was looking at life. It was liberating even to write down my emotions—good, bad, and indifferent—because they were up and down like a rollercoaster. By documenting that experience, I was able to bring closure to it. I was also able to look back at how far I had come, and it has been a reminder to me of a period in my life to which I never want to return. I was able to reflect on that period and say, "OK. Let me make sure I don't do that again, because this is what that experience was like." Journaling and documenting a process like this allows you not only to be liberated and free, and to bring closure, but it's a great opportunity to be able to reflect on it and then share some of those lessons learned and turn them into teachable moments for other people.

This is exactly what I intend to do with this book. I want to share the journey I went through and the experiences I had and the lessons I learned. I hope that they are helpful to you, just like I hope you're able to share what you've gone through with other people and be a help to them.

Tip #9: Explore New Avenues and New Streams of Income

You must look for other ways to generate income over and above your current salary. In times like these, you do not want to become totally dependent on plan A and on the current job you have. Look at the number of people who are now out of work who were dependent on that one job. We're in an age now when we no longer have employment contracts that guarantee us a job for life or until we retire. Look at your skills, gifts, talents, interests, and even your hobbies, and find ways that you can market them and turn them into an additional stream of income.

Many of us have a side hustle. I mentioned above that I am currently a chief diversity and inclusion officer and workplace strategist for an organization—but I also have a side hustle. I've turned my training and speaking and coaching skills into a business; I am always looking for opportunities to leverage these gifts and skills and to speak at different conferences that are not specific to my day job.

You have to look for specific opportunities to leverage your gifts and skills so that you have a backup plan, because ultimately your backup plan may become your plan A. You may even be able to work yourself out of your full-time day job by leveraging and building that skill set, those talents, those gifts, and those hobbies on the side, and turn them into a full-time job that you've been wanting to pursue all your life.

Your skill might be sewing; you might enjoy alterations. There are a lot of people out there looking for alterations people. Or, you might want to write short stories; or you may be really good at building things; or tinkering on cars—there are so many different things that you enjoy doing and that you're really good at. You've got to be able to tap into those talents and create that additional stream of income. And along with exploring those new avenues and new streams of income, you've got to continue to hone and develop yourself. I can't say enough about continuous learning—becoming a lifelong student. It might mean taking a class at night; it might mean reading books about a specific hobby that you enjoy; it might be learning about how to start your own business by going to the Small Business Administration and taking a couple of courses; it might be shadowing someone or finding a mentor in a specific trade that you're interested in.

When I was interested in getting into the professional speaking business, above and beyond what I do on a daily basis with my job, I went to people who were already in the speaking business. I joined organizations like the National Speakers Association so that I could learn the trade; so that I could be around the people; so that I could make contacts; and so that ultimately one day I could reach out and turn those contacts into contracts. Continuous learning is an extremely important part of creating that additional stream of income and leveraging your skills and your talents.

Tip #10: Celebrate and Reward Your Successes

Acknowledge your accomplishments and your progress. This is something that we don't do enough; but it's something that is important to do along the way. You should set up milestones for checking in and seeing how you're progressing; and you should celebrate those milestones that you reach successfully.

When you've reached the end of your journey, and you have finally come out of debt—How liberating that is! It's so important for you to celebrate that success. Not only do you want to document it in your journal, but you also want to pat yourself on the back. You may want to treat yourself to a nice dinner, or you may want to dress up and go hang out with some friends.

Celebrating your milestones doesn't mean getting back into debt by going out to buy another big-ticket item. Sometimes people do that. They get out of debt and now they want to reward themselves with this brand-new car that they've been eyeing. One of my friends told me that when she got out of debt she celebrated, but instead of buying a brand-new car she went and rented a beautiful, brand-new BMW for the day. It cost her $49 for the day. She had the opportunity to drive in her dream car and it gave her the motivation to continue on her journey until she reached the level where she felt she could afford something like that. What a noble and creative idea—and inexpensive—only $49! You may just want to do something small, but don't underestimate the power of personal affirmation. It's important to have the right people in your life—your mentor or financial coach or accountability partner. Have a great family dinner and celebrate the fact that you are now out of debt, because it's so important that you not only have that sense of accomplishment, but that you continue the journey.

Remember, now it becomes a lifestyle. It's not just something you did to check a box and say that you're done, and then you revert back to your old ways. This is now the way you want to live; it's part of your habits; it's part of your lifestyle; and you want to make sure

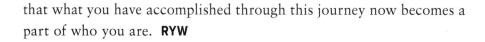

that what you have accomplished through this journey now becomes a part of who you are. **RYW**

Summary

- We're at a crossroad of change and we need to reposition and re-evaluate, redefine and refocus, repair and reestablish our financial management plan.
- It takes years to get into debt; getting out of debt isn't going to be an overnight miracle.
- The things we heard about money growing up, which were rein-forced from our childhood, into our adolescence and teenage years, and even into our adult years, are now shaping our habits.
- There are five principles for financial success: Assess your gifts and talents, nurture your gifts, create stable income for stable bills, determine what money is discretionary, and reach a zero balance. One more tip: a rise in income is not a permission to spend.
- Without a plan you fail. You need a step-by-step plan; you need to set financial goals; you need to create a weekly/monthly budget; and you need to have the right resources.
- Another critical element of creating a financial plan is saving money for unforeseen circumstances. And don't worry about what others think; you don't need their approval.
- Think beyond your day job, save money, don't lend money to family or friends, pay down those credit cards, and enjoy the liberating feel-ing you will have.
- Take advantage of financial opportunities such as 401(k) plans, health care flexibility plans, tuition reimbursement plans, life insur-ance, and training.
- Know your FICO score so you can track the effects of your efforts to restore your good credit rating.
- My Top Ten Tips for gaining financial stability:
  1. Establish Your Financial Situation
  2. Contact Your Creditors

3. Obtain a Copy of Your Credit Report
4. Prioritize What Bills You Pay Down First
5. Set Smart Goals
6. Make This a Family Affair
7. Review Your Goals
8. Journal Your Journey
9. Explore New Avenues and New Streams of Income
10. Celebrate and Reward Your Successes

Remember: The *Reinvent Yourself Workbook* provides exercises, reflection questions, and personal assessments based on the material presented in this chapter. WHEN YOU SEE THIS SYMBOL **RYW**, IT MEANS THAT THERE IS A CORRESPONDING EXERCISE OR ACTIVITY FOR YOU TO COMPLETE. Working these exercises will help you to better integrate the material and focus your efforts towards reinventing yourself and achieving success in moving to the next level in your life. Visit **www.drshirleydavis.com/store**.

■ CHAPTER EIGHT:
Reclaiming Your Personal Power

Take Control of Your Destiny

THIS ENTIRE BOOK HAS BEEN ABOUT CONTROLLING YOUR DESTINY—reclaiming your personal power and taking your life back. The process starts with you personally doing a self-assessment and identifying why you exist; what is your purpose; what are your strengths, gifts, and talents; taking into account your health and well-being; and then focusing on reinventing your career, your relationships, your finances, and every other area of your life.

The fact that we even need to reclaim our power means that we may have allowed someone else or something else to derail us, to distract us, or to disrupt us from being our best self. If so, who was it? Or what was it? And why did we allow that someone or that something to have that much power over us?

I've written about a number of situations in this book that consumed me for a period of time: going through a divorce, dealing with bad bosses, experiencing career setbacks, fighting my way out of a financial pit, and dealing with toxic relationships and toxic people. These situations took away my personal power by taking away my peace of mind, my money, my time, and at times, my will to go on.

Trouble is inevitable; but misery is optional. In many of those situations, I can remember being a basket-case. I couldn't concentrate; I couldn't think straight; I couldn't sleep; and I lost weight. I would curl up in the bed under the sheets; I didn't want to be around people; I didn't want to go anywhere; and I felt powerless. **RYW**

The message I have for you is what I finally had to say to myself during those difficult situations: Snap out of it! Get up. Shake the dust off your feet. Don't get bitter—get better! Stop giving your power away to people who are haters, people who are unimportant and insignificant, and to situations that are temporary and will ultimately pass anyway. You've got to channel your energy in a positive way and never allow anything to have that much control over you.

Someone once said: "He who controls others may be powerful, but he who has mastered himself is mightier still." The greatest revenge is success, and I have designed this book for precisely that reason: to help you achieve success in every area of your life. The fact that you're investing your time and money to make these motivational, inspirational, and practical strategies your own—to take your life to the next level—is a quantum leap in the right direction. You are to be commended.

As you head down this road and travel on this journey of reclaiming your personal power, I encourage you not to spend a whole lot of time thinking about who derailed you or who distracted you, or who you allowed to take control of your own personal power. Instead, I ask you to invest that time in thinking about WHY you allow other people to take that level of control.

Personal power is something we were all born with—we all have it. It's only when we choose to allow someone else to take that personal power that it impacts our lives. So I ask you simply to think about why you allow other people to come into your life, to control your happiness, to control your joy, and ultimately to control your destiny. **RYW**

Strategies for Reclaiming Your Personal Power

OK. After you've given that some thought, now shift your time and energy into learning how to reclaim your personal power. Throughout this entire book I've provided you with tips, strategies, and practices for what you can do to take your life to the next level, and what you can do to reinvent yourself. Many of those same strategies apply here as well; let me highlight a few that I think are relevant to reclaiming your personal power.

Leave the Past in the Past

Here's an important place to start: Make sure that you are leaving the past in the past. Don't keep holding on to something that you can't control or something that has already happened. It's behind you. You've got to move forward. And remember, sometimes you've got to die to who you've been to give birth to who you can become. **RYW**

Use Your Past Successes as Motivation

The second thing I recommend is that you recall past successes. Focus on those areas, whether big or small, in which you were successful. In the last chapter I emphasized the concept of "journaling your journey" and how important it is to document your experiences—the things you learned, and even your successes. Recall those experiences now; use them as fuel to motivate you for the future. Use them to help identify your dreams for the future, your goals, and your vision—whatever it's going to take to motivate you. That's what you want to recall. That's what I did. I had some successes, and I used those successes as a springboard for my future. **RYW**

Forgive Others

Another thing we have to do if we want to reclaim our personal power is to learn how to forgive. It's tough to do; it's very difficult. I had to work it out in a number of different situations and different disappointments with people who had hurt me in the past. If you harbor bitterness and resentment and unforgiveness, it will derail your success.

Remember: The *Reinvent Yourself Workbook* provides exercises, reflection questions, and personal assessments based on the material presented in this chapter. WHEN YOU SEE THIS SYMBOL **RYW**, IT MEANS THAT THERE IS A CORRESPONDING EXERCISE OR ACTIVITY FOR YOU TO COMPLETE. Working these exercises will help you to better integrate the material and focus your efforts towards reinventing yourself and achieving success in moving to the next level in your life. Visit **www.drshirleydavis.com/store**.

It will eat you up inside like a cancer. It can cause stress; it can cause anxiety and depression; and it can manifest itself in a number of other health issues.

Often, the person toward whom you're harboring unforgiveness either doesn't know it or they've moved on with their life. So you've got to do the same. You've got to let it go, no matter how much they hurt you, no matter how deep the wound, no matter how devastating the experience. Even if it was intentional, you still have to let it go, and you've got to channel that energy into something positive. **RYW**

Recognize Your Limitations

Next, I recommend that you recognize and own up to your own weaknesses and limitations. In order to reclaim your personal power, you've got to be honest with yourself. You've got to know what you can and can't do. Whenever you can, develop and turn your weaknesses into strengths; and when you can't, focus on what you CAN do. **RYW**

Stay in Your Own Lane

My fifth recommendation for reclaiming your personal power is to stay in your own lane. Stop trying to live your life for other people; stop trying to live your life through other people's eyes. You've got to live out your own purpose and your own vision. You need to dust off your own dream and start pursuing that dream. You can't live your life through the eyes of others. So stop measuring your life and comparing your life against someone else's; their life wasn't given to you to live, and your life wasn't given to them to live. Do not give other people that kind of power. When you don't know what you were created to do; when you don't know your purpose or your own vision, other people will define it for you; and not only will they define it, but they will also confine you with it. It will be very limiting.

The two most important moments in our lives are the day we were born and the day we realize why we were born. Wouldn't you hate to get to the point of death only to realize that you've never really lived?

Wouldn't you hate to realize that you never scraped the surface of your potential? What if you lived your whole life only to discover that it was all wrong—that you spent 40 hours a week for 35 years working in a job that you weren't even called to do? What if you realized that you were doing something that didn't really fulfill your purpose?

Remember, we are all born unique, but too many people die as a copy. Too many people die at age 30 but don't get buried until age 80. Can you imagine going through 50 years of your life aimlessly, meaninglessly, not understanding why you were born? Can you imagine not contributing, not adding value, and not having anything to show for the life that you lived?

I challenge you and I urge you to maximize and capitalize on the time that you've been given. Be satisfied with the life that you have. Be comfortable and even impressed with you—not in an arrogant way, but in a self-confident, building way. Nobody can beat you at being you. It's easy to be you. It takes a whole lot more effort to be somebody you're not meant to be. It takes a lot of energy to fake it, and you've got to tell a whole lot of lies. But when you are comfortable with yourself, and living in your own skin, and staying in your lane, then you can enjoy your life with truth and authenticity. And that is very liberating. **RYW**

Surround Yourself with the Right People

Next, and I can't stress this enough, reevaluate your relationships. Please go back and reread Chapter 6 on Reevaluating Your Relationships, because it's such a relevant aspect of reclaiming your personal power and taking your life back. Make sure that you are avoiding toxic people and toxic situations. In chapter 6 I addressed how important it is to surround yourself with the right people. Surround yourself with smart people—people who are smarter than you, who are more successful than you, and who are positive.

If you are a 10, and you're surrounded by 2's and 3's, you will not be a 10 for long. And if you are the smartest person in your group, you need to expand your group and bring in people who are smarter than you. Look at your closest friends; take an inventory, and ask yourself: "What are these relationships doing FOR me? What are they doing TO me?" Look for ways that you can begin to develop strategic relationships and strategic partners with people who have more than you, know more than you, have achieved a greater level of success, people who have been there/done that, and can help you learn and grow. **RYW**

Don't Assume the Victim Role

The next thing that I advise for taking back your life is that you choose not to be a victim. Do not allow yourself to assume the victim role; do not let yourself get into a self-defeatist attitude. Life is not what happens to you; life is what you do with what happens to you. Reclaiming your personal power is all about taking life's lessons and using them as a springboard to reach the next level. We have all experienced failure. Everybody plays the fool sometimes, right? Make the choice not to live on Victim Street, and find ways to get to Victory Boulevard. **RYW**

Conquer Your Fears

Do not let yourself be paralyzed by fear, whether it's fear of failure, fear of getting hurt, fear of looking stupid, and certainly not fear of success. Many people fear success because it takes a toll getting there, and then it takes an even greater toll to maintain that level of success. The best way to conquer fear, first of all, is to just try. Write down the things that you fear the most; and then identify why you fear those things. Fear is a learned behavior; it's also something you can conquer and overcome. Write down those things that you fear the most; write down what you would do in the event that your worst fears happened. Eighty-five percent of the things we worry about never happen. So do not sabotage your own dreams and your own vision and your own success because you fear—something. **RYW**

Invest in Yourself

If you're going to take your life back, if you're going to reach the next level, you've got to find ways to increase your knowledge. Knowledge is not just power, knowledge is the new currency. While most people are focused on the general economy, I encourage you to focus on your personal economy. You've got to learn new things, generate new ideas, build new skills, expand your mindset, and broaden your exposure. Expose yourself to new people, new things, and different cultures and places. Try things that you haven't tried before. Go places where you haven't gone before.

People tend to get into a rut; they get into their comfort zone and they want to stay there. I encourage you to step outside your comfort zone and try those things that you haven't tried in the past. Success is a choice. But success is also a learned behavior—just like failure is a learned behavior. You've got to be willing to do the things today that others won't do in order to have the things tomorrow that others won't have. **RYW**

Be Grateful—and Optimistic

My final tip and my parting gift as I conclude this book on reinventing yourself is this: As you reclaim your personal power, always maintain an attitude of gratitude. Attitude is everything; as I said before, your attitude determines your altitude. And I believe that the best attitude is one of gratitude. I urge you and I encourage you to always be grateful for your life, for the experiences that life has brought you, the lessons that you've learned, the people who have crossed your path, and those individuals who will be there forever.

May you always be appreciative of the simple things in life that we take for granted every day: the breath that we take, the air that we breathe, the movement of our limbs, the sunny days, and even the rainy days. And may you appreciate the rainbow that comes after the rain, be grateful for the opportunity to have dinner with family and special friends, and enjoy special moments like holidays, birthdays, and anniversaries.

May you always be mindful of how precious every day is, and recognize that yesterday will never come again, that tomorrow is not promised, and that today is a gift—that's why it's called the present (smile). We all have 24 hours in a day. What we do with them is up to us. So as you reinvent yourself, and as you take this journey toward stepping into your greatness, may you find peace, fulfillment, and joy in every area of your life—and may all your dreams come true. **RYW**

Summary

- Reclaiming your personal power and taking your life back starts with you personally doing a self-assessment and identifying why you exist, what is your purpose, what are your strengths, your gifts, and your talents.
- Snap out of it! Get up. Shake the dust off your feet. Don't get bitter—get better!
- Relevant tips, strategies, and practices for what you can do to reinvent yourself and take your life to the next level. Let me highlight the ten most relevant strategies:
  1. Leave the Past in the Past
  2. Use Your Past Successes as Motivation
  3. Forgive Yourself and Others
  4. Recognize Your Limitations
  5. Stay in Your Own Lane
  6. Surround Yourself with the Right People
  7. Don't Assume the Victim Role
  8. Conquer Your Fears
  9. Invest in Yourself
  10. Be Grateful—and Optimistic
- Every day is a gift. What you do with it is up to you.

▪▪ About the Author

DR. SHIRLEY DAVIS, SPHR, AFFECTIONATELY KNOWN AS The Success Doctor™, is an accomplished corporate executive, global workforce management expert, an international speaker, and executive coach. She is President of SDS Enterprises, a global workforce solutions firm that provides strategies and solutions for how to work, lead, and succeed in a global, virtual, diverse, and hyper-connected world. She has worked in 10 countries as a consultant, speaker, and facilitator.

She has over 25 years of business and human resources experience and has worked at several Fortune 500 companies in various senior and executive leadership roles including Bank of America, Circuit City Stores, Capital One, Constellation Energy, and more recently, as Vice President of Global Diversity & Inclusion and Workplace Strategies. She has been featured and quoted on NBC's The Today Show, in the *Wall Street Journal, Essence Magazine, Black Enterprise Magazine, The Washington Post, HR Magazine,* and CNN.com and has been honored with numerous awards. She's currently co-authoring several new books, *"Stepping Stones to Success,"* featuring Deepak Chopra, Jack Canfield, and other experts and *"Leadership: Helping Others to Succeed,"* to be released later this year.

She was named one of the Top 100 Corporate Executives in America by *Uptown Professional Magazine* four consecutive years (2011-2014). In 2011, she was named as a 2012 "Woman Worth Watching" by *Profiles in Diversity Journal* and she received the "Strategic Star" Award by *Diversity Woman Magazine* in Dec. 2012, and was honored with the Catalyst Award in 2013 by *Uptown Professional.*

She holds a Bachelor's in Pre-Law; a Master's in HR Management; and a Ph.D. in Business and Organization Management, with a specialization in Leadership. She's also a certified Senior Human Resources professional (SPHR), and currently pursuing her Certified Speaking Professional designation (CSP) with the National Speaker's Association. She's a former Miss District of Columbia, Mrs. Oklahoma, Ms. Virginia, and in 2000 won the national title of Ms. American United States. She serves on several boards is very active in her community and her church.

Dr. Davis resides in the Washington, Metro DC area with her husband of three years, Terrell Sheppard, and their three children, Gabrielle Victoria, Brian, and Terra.

For more information on Dr. Shirley Davis visit her website at www.drshirleydavis.com.

Praise From Clients and Colleagues For The Author

"Dr. Davis is a well-known and highly-respected personality and subject matter expect in the field of business. In that regard she carries herself with the utmost professionalism and dignity and whenever she shares her expertise, my colleagues and I are assured of the best of quality."

Uptown Professional Magazine

Dr. Shirley Davis is one of the most dynamic and captivating speakers I've seen on stage. She's humorous, full of energy, and keeps people fully engaged and on the edge of their seats. As she shares her real life personal stories, setbacks, strategies, and solutions, she inspires, empowers and motivates others to achieve greatness and to go to the next level. And I'm proud to call her a member of the Les Brown Speaker's Network.

Speech Coach, Les Brown, International Motivational Speaker

Dr. Davis has been my success and career coach for the past three years. Each month I look forward to her inspiration, and practical tips on how I can improve my life, not just my career. From the first session, I knew that I had to have her in my life. And over the years, I have been promoted twice and increased my self-confidence.

Coaching Client

As a speaker, Dr. Davis has the ability to connect with her audiences, through enlightened, passionate and dynamic delivery. Dr. Davis' words challenge, inspire, uplift and motivate. Whether speaking in front of hundreds or in smaller intimate groups, Dr. Davis brings authenticity and personality In her delivery. Highly recommended.

Corporate Client

"Dr. Davis spoke at our convention this year and she was one of the highest rated speakers we've had in a long time. The audience hung on her every word. She had us laughing, taking copious notes, and learning new strategies that I plan to use in my daily work. In fact, she had to stay an hour afterwards to accommodate the long line of attendees waiting to greet her. This has never happened in our company training programs. Thanks Dr. Davis"

Corporate Client

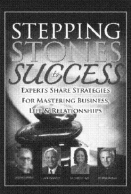
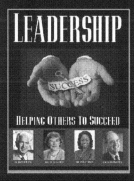